Still More GEMS

Still More GEMS

*12-Step Shares,
Notes and Thoughts*

Andy C.

ISBN: 9781990446092 (KDP Softcover)
ISBN: 9781990446108 (Ingram Hardcover)
ISBN: 9781990446115 (Ingram Softcover)
ISBN: 9781990446122 (Digital)

Contents

Introduction

This is the third collection of GEMS, meditations on recovery in the Fellowship of AA. I write these books, publish weekly blogs and podcasts, and provide a recovery-oriented website with supporting materials and essays for the AA community and anyone interested in recovery. My purpose in all of this is "to engender and enhance spiritual growth."

Spiritual maintenance and, by implication, growth, is the hallmark of our AA fellowship, and this is my contribution. I hope they help you. I know producing them has helped me.

Now, as ever the lawyer I feel compelled to include a caveat: These are only my thoughts; take what you can use and leave the rest behind.

PART ONE

The Pandemic

The great COVID-19 plague started in the fall of 2019.

Plagues are a fearful phenomenon; they evoke and trigger a deep and dramatic response in humans. Our reaction to infectious diseases is instinctive; a (human) race fear that we all feel.

The fear is so deep, we could call it spiritual. Anxiety rises from our subconscious; we cannot be protected from this invisible, silent, harmful agent. In the early days, with little or no information, we fill in the worst case and unconsciously frame it as an implacable malevolent foe.

It is a truth of all plagues that fear drives the agenda. On a personal level, fear for ourselves spawns a hundred forms of negative behaviours. Fear for the safety of children leads parents to extreme lengths. Behaviours considered rude in normal times become normal. Within societies, divisions of opinion, driven by fear, are clear and enforced loudly.

We AAs know about fear. We may not understand it, but we know it. And we have learned to rely on a Higher Power to deal with it. AA responded to this pandemic and its plague of fear; we changed how we did business. In-person meetings were cancelled, personal contact was lost, and face-to-face fellowship opportunities vanished. But the AA Fellowship quickly found new ways to engage with itself and newcomers.

Dealing with newcomers was more critical than ever, as the stresses and strains of the plague exacerbated addictive tendencies in the drinking class. One AA, interviewed on the radio was asked, "Do you think the lockdowns and the COVID waves are causing more alcoholism?"

Our AA friend replied, "I am not sure that the lockdowns are causing more alcoholism, but they reveal more alcoholics. And we in AA are ready, willing and able to help them."

These are some GEMS written during the time of the COVID plague.

Newcomer at an Online Meeting

It was early in the COVID panic, our regular men's Tuesday night meeting was online.

The electronic meeting room opened early. We enjoyed a pre-meeting meeting, catching up on personal news and cracking rude jokes. It was the usual banter and humour of AA brothers.

In the midst of our laughter, a new face and name appeared among the picture tiles on our computer screens.

It was an older man. He was sitting at his desk. Over his shoulder, a young lady was working on the keyboard of his computer. When satisfied that she had successfully signed in, she looked directly into the webcam and said, "I know this is a meeting for men only; I am just setting my father up. This is his first meeting with Alcoholics Anonymous, and it is long overdue. He is helpless with computers, so I set him up; now I will leave."

Then she turned to the older man and said in a tone that cut off any disagreement, "Okay, you are in the meeting. Sit here, listen and learn."

She turned back to the webcam and said, "Goodbye!"

She turned and walked away, pausing at the door of the room, still in the camera frame, she said to our newcomer, "I'll be back in an hour," then left and shut the door.

We all watched our screens. One of the guys said, "Welcome! Was the young lady right? Is this your first meeting?"

"Yes," came the cautious reply, "I have never been to one of these meetings. I hope it is okay that I just show up like this."

He continued, looking at his screen rather than the webcam, "My daughter caught me drinking this morning; we had a bit of a confrontation. She decided I needed to get in touch with AA. She called your central office and set me up for this meeting. As you heard, she can be firm. So, here I am."

It was a great meeting. We got his name and his contact information. We gave him our names as well. One of the guys delivered a Big Book the following day, and we assigned him to a temporary sponsor. A successful introduction to AA. And by the way, as I write this, he is four weeks sober and attending four meetings a week.

When this pandemic hit, we pivoted to online meetings and kept the bridges to sobriety open. This took effort, and we had to work at it. Thank goodness we did.

Some of our AA brothers and sisters don't like online meetings, complaining that "it's just not the same." They keep in touch by calling around and talking with their friends in AA. This is good. But calling around and keeping in touch amongst ourselves does nothing for the newcomer who shows up, with the aid of his computer-savvy daughter.

A New Normal

Many commentators on the pandemic have said, "We have a new normal."

Let's unpack this phrase. *Normal*: A noun, meaning a usual, typical, or expected state or condition. *New*: An adjective, meaning discovered recently or realized for the first time; not existing before; already existing but seen, experienced or acquired recently, or now for the first time.

The commentators were right; with the pandemic, we developed new normals. We immediately accustomed ourselves to several feet of separation in lines; local restaurants had tables on the sidewalks, and they offered ready-to-serve take-a-way meals. In no time, we were all washing our hands more than ever and avoiding coughing anywhere. These practices and habits were new, and they quickly became routine. Within a short time, we had a new normal.

Pandemics are not the only cause of new normals. In AA rooms, we often hear, "When we sober up, we have a new normal."

When I sobered up, I developed new habits like attending meetings when I felt disturbed, calling my sponsor before making decisions and reading AA and other spiritual books. These habits became my normal; I established a new normal.

For both pandemics and sobriety, we find new normals.

And note, we don't refer to this change of state as the *last normal* or the *final normal*. There was an old normal, and there will be a future normal. We describe our current state as a new one, knowing it will, in due course, become an old one.

In the case of the pandemic, someday, the current panic will pass, and we will have a future new normal. Some of the pandemic's habits, our current new normal, may carry forward into our future normal. Restaurants may still have sidewalk tables, and we may continue to wash our hands frequently.

And this is true in sobriety as well. In AA, as we grow, we establish new normals. My sobriety in year one differed from year five and again for years ten, twenty and forty. Habits changed, and new normals were created when I worked the Steps, and practiced the principles of the Program in all my affairs. Each new normal has been succeeded by a future normal, with some habits from the last new normal carried forward and some lost.

The great plague of 2019 triggered new normals. Likewise, sobering up began a new normal. And over the years of practicing the Steps, I find there are old normals, new normals, and there will be future normals. That is the nature of a well-maintained spiritual life.

Persistence

When I successfully practice Program principles, I am on the beam. I am easier to work with in the office, my wife sees a better me, and my tennis partner sees a calmer me.

But, I am not always on the beam. My workmates will sometimes see that I am afraid; my wife will sometimes hear an irritated, snippy tone in my voice; and I still lose my temper on the tennis court.

When I fall short, I cause damage, and amends must be made. I drag myself back to the Program principles; it feels like I am muscling my way back to the beam, like I have a persistence muscle, and it is getting a workout.

I sweat and strain in a good fitness workout, and my muscles emerge more robust and improved. And occasionally, I have a double-hard workout. It hurts, but the pain has a gain; I am fitter.

In normal times, my persistence muscle gets a daily workout. And in these times of COVID panic, the workouts are more intense; it seems I am putting my persistence muscle through a double hard workout.

In this time of panic, my persistence muscle is getting a double-hard workout and will emerge more robust and improved.

The Alcoholic Advantage

Alcoholics have an advantage over normal folk.

Here are a couple of stories to demonstrate this.

I was talking with a non-AA business acquaintance. He complained about a recent conversation that had not gone well. While talking with another fellow, he made a minor criticism, and the other man exploded in rage.

I paused, unconsciously framing the problem within Program parameters. I replied, "It sounds like fear was dominating him, and he lashed out. Eventually, you will have to forgive him."

My acquaintance looked at me like I was an idiot. "Where would you get that idea? Forgive him, no way, ... he was just an asshole, and I'll never deal with him again."

My acquaintance had lost a valuable business connection.

Another example: An AA friend tells the story of a luncheon with a business associate. Over lunch, his associate complained bitterly about his staff, clients, and everything else in his world. My AA friend, forgetting he was talking with a Normie, said, "When I get into an angry frame of mind, where nothing seems to be working out the way I want, I have to take stock, do a personal inventory."

His non-AA friend looked at him like he had a third eye and dismissed him with a "Yeah, whatever."

At last report, his associate was still suffering.

We have an AA advantage; we can deal with things that used to baffle us, and these things that baffle us are no different from the things that confuse many of the Normies around us. But we have an advantage, we have tools, and we have spent a lot of time working on ourselves. Moreover, we have listened to shares in the rooms and had conversations with fellow AAs that have taught us many do's and don'ts of life. We have observed many examples of solutions, both good and bad.

And we are compelled to do this, or we die.

This advantage becomes more apparent in a crisis; we know what to do. When a pandemic unfolds, we know what to do to keep calm, poised, and serene. We have a playbook, Steps we can follow.

We have Program friends we can lean on. We can meditate more, pray more, and keep in touch more.

Acquiring this AA advantage was not easy. We have faced demons, fears, and dependencies. But as a result, we have greater self-awareness and control. And some of us have been blessed with confidence in the universe that transcends faith.

In these perilous times, we can demonstrate victory over our troubles so that others can see the strength of our way of life.

Here's a great article on 12-Step living in times of crisis: https://www.psychologytoday.com/us/blog/why-we-need-heroes/202003/how-the-wisdom-12-step-programs-can-help-get-us-through-april

Faith Trumps Fear

We just finished our Thursday meeting. During this time of the pandemic, the meeting was online.

To start the meeting, we read Chapter Three of the Twelve and Twelve. It was a reading about AAs and their spiritual dependence during a crisis. Here it is:

" When World War II broke out, this spiritual principle (of dependence on a Power greater than ourselves) had its first major test. AAs entered the services and were scattered all over the world. Would they be able to take discipline, stand up under fire, and endure the monotony and misery of war? Would the kind of dependence they had learned in AA carry them through? Well, it did. They had even fewer alcoholic lapses, or emotional binges than AAs safe at home did. They were just as capable of endurance and valor as any other soldiers. Whether in Alaska or on the Salerno beachhead, their dependence upon a Higher Power worked. And far from being a weakness, this dependence was their chief source of strength."

Let me paraphrase the reading and frame it in the context of the current COVID panic:

" When the worldwide pandemic broke out in 2020, our spiritual principle (of dependence on a power greater than ourselves) had a major test. AAs were scattered all over the world. Would they be able to take discipline, stand up under fire, and endure the monotony of lockdowns and misery of the pandemic? Would the kind of dependence they had learned in AA carry them through? Well, it did. They had fewer alcoholic lapses than ever; and fewer emotional binges than others. They were just as capable of endurance and valor as any other citizen. Wherever they were, AAs responded with love and compassion. Far from being a weakness, spiritual dependence was their chief and growing source of strength."

This paraphrase is apt. Fear is part of the human and AA condition.

During World War II, AAs survived and thrived in the fear and anxiety of that time. Not only did they thrive and survive, but they also improved their relationship with their Higher Power. So, too, in this time of virus panic, we survive and thrive. And more than merely thrive; we improved our relationship with each other and our Higher Power.

We kept in touch and reached out to new-comers and anyone who needed help. Many in the Fellowship increased their habits of prayer and meditation. With online meetings, we met new friends from around the world. And AAs turned more and more to their Higher Power for strength.

And when the plague passes, we will have a more profound and robust sense of "God, as we understood Him."

We will have added a new chapter to our personal story with God and increased our dependence upon Him.

PART TWO

Excitement and Apathy

Many stories told in the rooms of AA revolve around themes of excitement or apathy. The frequency of these themes in alcoholic stories suggests that we alcoholics are attracted to both apathy and excitement. This is a paradox. Excitement would seem to be the opposite of apathy and vice versa. But observing the frequency and attraction to both, it does not seem a stretch to say we are addicted to them.

Alcoholics spend a lot of time being excited and doing exciting things. And if life does not present us with enough excitement, we look for it, and, if we cannot find it, we create it. We may be addicted to excitement.

We forget to remember the things that kept us sober. We become comfortable and ignore that which brought us comfort. We experience moments of serenity and take them for granted, forgetting the self-examination, prayer, and meditation that made those moments possible. We may be addicted to apathy.

These are some meditations on our two loves, excitement and apathy.

Excitement and Happy

One of the topics at an AA meeting was happiness.

An AA brother shared a few stories from his drinking days. The litany of events included fights, arrests, and general mayhem. Tales that would have shamed a normal person but were amusing to alcoholic ears.

He paused, "oddly, all these troubles kept me drinking. I was afraid of a sober life. I thought I was happy and a life without drinking would be unhappy. The sober people I knew did not get into fights and did not get arrested. Their lives were not exciting. And without excitement, they could not be happy.

    But I had to stop drinking; it was killing me. I resigned myself to a life of unhappiness.

I shared this fear with my sponsor, who told me his story.

One weekend early in his sobriety, his wife insisted on a picnic with their children. He did not look forward to it; he thought the idea of a picnic was deadly dull. He went but complained all the way.

After a great lunch, he relaxed and watched his children play. He experienced a strange emotion. It was not unpleasant, but it was decidedly odd. Worried, he described this unfamiliar feeling to his wife.

According to my sponsor, she smiled and told him that the feeling sounded like happiness. Then she pointed out that family picnics did not create excitement but did create happiness.

My sponsor had confused happiness with excitement.

He would have thanked his wife for this insight, but that would have cost him relationship points in his marriage.

Because I was not married to my sponsor, I could thank him for the insight without losing relationship points."

Important Metric
of Importance

"If it's important, I find a way; if it's not important, I find an excuse."

This aphorism was a topic for our AA meeting. As the discussion unfolded, we saw that excuses were a warning sign. A warning sign we ignored at our peril.

The fellow who tabled this topic for discussion had returned to the Rooms after a slip; he admitted, "When I sobered up, the Program was important. I found a way to get to meetings, I found a way to keep in touch with the guys, and I found a way to pray and meditate. Then things got good; I was making more money, my family was off my back, and my job improved.

I become complacent; my sobriety became less and less important. And as my Program became less important, I found fewer *ways* to pay attention to spiritual maintenance and more *excuses* to avoid working the Program.

Instead of finding a way to go to meetings, I found excuses to miss them. Rather than finding a way to keep in touch with fellow alcoholics, I found excuses to avoid them. I had always found a way to work on the Steps, but now I found excuses to avoid the work. I replaced finding a way to pray and meditate with excuses for not meditating and not praying."

He summarized:

" Losing touch with the importance of sobriety, I went back out.

I have been drinking heavily for some time and am back, back at Step One. The Program is important again; I know this because I find *ways* instead of looking for *excuses*. More ways, fewer excuses, that is the key.

And if I see more excuses than ways, a red light starts flashing in my head; I pay more attention to spiritual maintenance."

What an incredible new insight and tool. I knew that when things became less important, I found excuses rather than ways. But this share introduced a new tool for my toolbox, the *excuses:ways ratio* as a measuring stick of importance.

Finding ways to do something instead of excuses to avoid something is more than truth; it is a benchmark and reality check.

If I notice myself making more excuses to avoid prayer, meditation, and self-examination, and finding fewer ways to practice these habits, my *excuses:ways ratio* is trending badly. It is proof my spiritual maintenance program is becoming less and less important. It is time to change course and direction back to the Program. It is a wake-up call to make my sobriety more important.

As we say about drinking, excuses are but a symptom.

Easy and Soft vs. Pain and Hard

When we read "How It Works," we are cautioned about easier, softer ways.

"Many of us thought we could find an easier, softer way." Followed by the warning, "We could not."

There is great truth in this caution: Don't take shortcuts to avoid the work which the Program demands.

But this caution does not mean the Program is the more difficult path to follow; although the work is hard, the Program is the easier, softer way.

At an AA meeting, we heard from a fellow who was "coming back."

He reported that he had been sober for several months and went back out. He continued his story, "I was sober and became complacent. Life got easier, and I lost touch with the solution. It seemed easier to duck meetings, avoid calling my sponsor; to sleep in rather than get up for a morning meditation."

He shook his head ruefully and continued:

" It seemed easier at the time. But boy, was I wrong.

I started drinking again and lost my job, home, and family.

To get desperate enough to come back and work the Program, I had to lose everything. And that is not an easier, softer way.

It is obvious to me now that working the Program would have been the easier, softer way. Drinking and losing everything is the difficult and harder way to get the motivation to work the Program."

We all learned from his pain. Losing everything to become desperate enough to make sobriety important is harder and more difficult.

Paradoxically, doing the hard work of the Program is the easier and softer way.

Spiritual Oasis

Water is essential if a man is dying of thirst in the desert. When he comes upon an oasis, he is overjoyed. The water and shade from the palms are a welcome relief.

In the beginning, he stays close to the oasis. But after his thirst is satisfied, the surge of joy subsides, and he feels free to wander away.

Away from the oasis, without water and exposed to the sun, he becomes thirsty and overheated. He runs back to the oasis. After a time at the oasis, thirst quenched, he wanders away till the sun and thirst drive him back. The cycle repeats.

One day, rested, cooled and unthirsty, he stays by the oasis. Instead of wandering, he begins to build a home. He breaks the thirst-recover-wander-thirst cycle and makes a life in the shade by the water. He begins to grow near the life-giving waters.

When I first sobered up, the pain was fresh; finding AA, I was overjoyed. I stayed near the Fellowship and my spiritual maintenance program.

The pain passed, and I wandered away from my spiritual habits. Exposed to life, I became restless and irritable, and this drove me back to my program. After a time, refreshed and restored, I wandered again. The cycle repeated.

One day, feeling content and mildly serene, instead of wandering away, I stayed. I stayed and paid attention to spiritual maintenance. I meditated, prayed and examined myself. With a daily meditation practice, I became more serene; by developing prayer habits, I found courage; by conducting self-examinations, my character improved.

I stopped the pain-wander-pain cycle. Like the desert traveler, I was building a home near the life-giving source. I was breaking the cycle of pain-growth-pain, and creating a spiritual home.

In the beginning, pain was a touchstone of growth. But one day, I grew without pain. Pain had become a stepping stone to growth.

Complacency Is Worse Than Resentment, #1

Years ago, I had a cable TV show.

I learned the importance of, "Hey Marthas."

"Hey, Marthas" are factoids that are surprising, interesting and grab your attention.

Imagine Henry, Martha's husband. He is in the living room, watching the news on TV. Martha is making supper in the kitchen. Henry sees and hears something—something that is so surprising and interesting, he calls out to his wife, "Hey, Martha, come here, you gotta see this." TV newsmen love "Hey, Marthas," they improve ratings.

Here are some "Hey Marthas":

- Patients do not fill 30% of prescriptions issued. Patients take the time to see a doctor and listen to him but don't finish the job by going to the drug store and filling the prescription.

- More than half of the medical patients who are given simple treatment regimens fail to start. And if they start, they rarely complete the recommended course of treatment; people don't follow through.

- In a hypertension study, 50% of the patients dropped out of a prescribed maintenance program. A prescribed program which immediately improved their lives. Even after people experienced positive results, one-half discontinued their treatments.

- In a cholesterol medication study, 40% of the patients stopped taking their medications after two years. Even with the threat of a heart attack, people won't stay the course.

Medical experts have a name for this; it is called *adherence*. Books have been written about adherence; it is a big problem. And it is a strange problem; people don't follow treatments that will save them. Despite feeling significant benefits, people fail to follow directions. Despite their awareness of significant health risks, people discontinue protocols and treatments. People fail to adhere.

We have the same problem in AA. We have an adherence problem.

Members become complacent. Though they see and feel the benefits of this new way of life and are fully aware of the deadly risks if they fail to adhere to the Program. They drop the habits that got them sober. They stop going to meetings, lose touch with their sponsors, and finally wander off.

For medical patients, lack of adherence is a leading cause of health problems. For alcoholics, lack of adherence is a leading cause of death and insanity.

Hey Martha, come here, you gotta hear this, "In AA, resentments might be the number one offender, but adherence is the number one problem."

Complacency Is Worse Than Resentment, #2

In the last GEM, I shared a series of "Hey Marthas" about patients not following medically prescribed treatments and protocols and compared those adherence problems to complacency in AA.

Doctors call it adherence; we call it staying with the Program. Medical experts see a lack of adherence; sponsors see sponsees drifting away from the Program.

If AAs and doctors share an adherence problem, maybe we share an adherence solution.

Medical experts have researched, tested, and reviewed ways to combat the problem of adherence.

They learned adherence improves with reminders. Small nudges are very effective. Medical people use simple phone and text reminders. And the improvement is magnified if there is a two-way communication between the patient and the medical professional, even if it is brief. And positive affirmations improve results; messages of "Well done" increase adherence.

In AA, we have small nudges to improve adherence, texts to remind newbies of meetings, calling them, and teaching them how to use a phone. And as medical professionals have found, even brief two-way communications will magnify the positive effect. We applaud at meetings for chips and service work, affirming good actions.

There is much power in small things.

Alcoholics are not unique. We are like medical patients with poor adherence, we are recovering alcoholics who become complacent. And like the medical community, the AA community has developed techniques and habits to improve adherence and combat complacency.

The solutions are there, and they are not complicated, but they do require some discipline.

PART THREE

Style and Fashion in Our Fellowship

Here are some GEMS tied to threads, fabrics, looms, and clothing. Fabrics and clothing are rich sources of metaphors and materials of life.

The Fabric of Your Life

Life is like fabric, woven with many threads.

I imagine my life as weaving cloth on a loom. I am the weaver, sitting at the loom. In front of me, vertical warp threads are pulled tight on the frame. I pass the shuttle with the weft threads back and forth. After each pass of the shuttle, I press the pedal on the loom. With a clatter, the loom tightens the threads, and I am ready to pass the shuttle in the opposite direction. With each pass, another strand of weft is woven into the warp, and a small amount of cloth is created.

With each pass of the shuttle, another thread is woven into the cloth. Looking at a single thread, I cannot see the design of colors and textures of the cloth on the loom. But thread by thread, a picture emerges.

From a basket beside me, I select threads to be woven. Together, the various threads that I choose to weave into the fabric create the design.

Warp and weft, the threads of the cloth, are the threads of life. Daily thoughts and actions are the passes of the shuttle, weaving the weft life threads into the warp life threads.

Woven together, the warp and weft threads reveal the design of my life.

The warp life threads are preset on the loom; I did not choose them; they were on the loom. These preset warp threads, which are stretched on the loom, include parents, home, health, and other circumstances. None of these were chosen by me, and all are beyond my control.

Unlike the warp threads, the threads of the weft are threads chosen by me. They are my decisions and matters over which I have control.

For example, my allergic reaction to alcohol is a warp thread. I did not select this thread, it was preset on the loom; it was a condition I was born with. But I chose to drink, and my choice to drink was a weft thread, a thread which I selected and wove into the warp threads with my metaphorical shuttle.

Deciding to drink was one thread I chose to incorporate into the fabric. Other weft threads which I selected were my thinking, perceptions, and attitudes. Each day, I chose them and wove them into my preset warp threads, family, intelligence and other things beyond my control.

When I came to AA, I stopped weaving the drinking thread into the fabric of my life and life improved. As a result, the now sober fabric design was much improved.

But I was still selecting other suboptimal weft threads as my shuttle continued back and forth. Threads like my old thinking, old perceptions, and old attitudes, threads which antedated my sobriety, were within easy reach, and I selected them. Though sober, I was still weaving anger, power driving, selfishness, and a hundred forms of fear into the cloth.

Over time I learned that self-centred thinking, self-pity, and resentment were all areas that needed a good thread-cleaning.

New threads, like love, prayer and meditation, were incorporated into the fabric. Changing old threads for new ones, I was weaving harmonious designs.

The first weft thread I dealt with was drinking, I still had the warp thread of an allergic reaction, but life did not include drinking and the fabric was better. But Step Twelve includes all the weft threads I choose to go into the weave, to create the fabric design.

Threads of AA History

The Oxford Group is woven into the fabric of AA.

One Oxford Group historical thread, well known to AAs, is the connection of Bill Wilson to the Oxford Group. That thread started with Carl Jung, who prescribed a spiritual experience to Rowland Hazard. Rowland Hazard filled the prescription by joining the Oxford Group. He and some Oxford Group friends rescued Ebby Thacher. Ebby grabbed hold of the Oxford Group ideas. As part of his Oxford Group work, he called on Bill Wilson.

That thread connecting the Oxford Group to Bill Wilson led to the creation of AA as we know it. It became part of the fabric of AA.

The Oxford Group's connection to Dr. Bob is equally important; it is the second Oxford Group thread woven into the fabric of AA. The story of this thread bears repeating.

Akron was home to the Firestone Tire Company. Mr. Firestone had a business problem; he needed talent for his company. He was impressed by an

Oxford Group leader, Mr. Newton, and brought him to Akron, hoping to recruit him as a senior manager.

Mr. Firestone had another problem. This second problem was personal. His son, Bud Firestone, was an alcoholic. Bud Firestone was Mr. Newton's age and, when Mr. Newton came to Akron, they became friends. Under Mr. Newton's influence, Bud sobered up. Mr. Firestone's affection for Mr. Newton and the Oxford Group soared, and this high-profile recovery enhanced the reputation of the Oxford Group in Akron.

Firestone Sr. became a major Oxford Group supporter and organized events to promote the Oxford Group. One event was a dinner introducing Oxford Group leaders to the great and good of Akron.

Henrietta Seiberling (of Seiberling Rubber Company fame) bought a table for dinner and she invited two couples to join her. One was T. Henry Williams and his wife, Claryce, and the other was Dr. Bob Smith and his wife, Anne.

Dr. Bob and T. Henry Williams met at the dinner. They became friends and, with Henrietta, formed an Oxford Group, holding regular meetings at the Williams home.

Dr. Bob admitted to the Group he had a drinking problem, which became a favorite topic of discussion for the Group. At one meeting in the spring of 1935, Henrietta led a Group prayer meeting, focusing on Dr. Bob's drinking. Three days later, Bill Wilson, at the suggestion of Rev. Tunks, called Henrietta and asked if she knew anyone with a drinking problem. Convinced that God had sent Bill in answer to the Group prayers, Henrietta called Anne Smith, who dragged Dr. Bob over to meet with Bill.

Bill met Bob. They started sobering up other drunks and held weekly meetings of the "Alcoholic Squad of the Oxford Group" at the home of T. Henry and Claryce Williams.

We should be grateful for both the Bill Wilson-Oxford Group thread and the Dr. Bob-Oxford Group thread. They are both important in the fabric of AA.

Inadequate Clothing

If you visit Scotland, you are not there because of the weather. Scottish weather is notoriously bad. It can involve "horizontal rain," which is pretty much as it sounds. And Scotland is famous for its thick wool sweaters. There is a good reason for this; you need thick wool sweaters to keep warm in the damp cold.

One rainy day in Edinburgh, we were eating at a restaurant. The couple at the table next to us asked the waitress, "Is the weather always this bad?"

With a broad Scottish accent, she said, "There is no such thing as bad weather; there is, however, inadequate clothing."

We all laughed.

The next day we went to a museum which was far out of our way. Because it was so far afield, we checked to ensure it was open. But when we arrived, the doors were locked. The note on the door read, "Closed early." The staff had left and locked up before the advertised closing time.

Irritated, I muttered, "Damn it, probably another Scottish labor dispute."

My dear wife said, in her best Scottish accent, "There is no such thing as bad events in life, but there are, however, inadequate attitudes."

I had to laugh. It was a rueful laugh but, to my credit, I did laugh.

The more I reflected on this idea of inadequate clothing in bad weather, analogous to inadequate attitudes when bad things happen, the more appropriate it seemed. Attitudes are the spiritual clothing for life. If I have a good attitude, whatever happens, I either take no notice or laugh it off. Attitudes are spiritual garments.

When I practice our Twelve Step principles in all my affairs, I acquire better and more adequate spiritual clothing.

We Dress Up

Recently my wife asked, "Does this sweater make me look fat?"

I gave the only answer possible, "No, it looks to me like you are losing weight."

"Well," she replied, "the scales show otherwise."

Rather than continue a discussion that could not possibly end well for me, I replied, "Well, it must be what you are wearing; never underestimate the value of a good tailor."

That concluded the conversation.

When we dress up and wear suitable clothing, our good features look better and our bad features less bad. We dress up to highlight our positives and mask our negatives to look better and feel better about ourselves.

In the same way, we dress up our behaviors. We dress up our actions and behaviors to highlight our positives and mask our negatives, so we look better and feel better about ourselves.

I think of a fellow at an AA meeting. He had a couple of months of sobriety.

The topic of the meeting was "Family life, now that we were sober."

He shared, "I am experiencing the benefits of the program already. I am helping my wife around the house more than I have ever helped before. I am finally carrying my share of the housework load. My wife is, I am sure, grateful for this Program; I know I am."

After the meeting, we went for coffee. We all agreed that it was terrific that he was carrying his share of all the household chores. Curious, one of the guys asked what he was doing.

He said with pride, "After my wife asked me, I put my underwear in the laundry hamper."

We all nodded in approval. Though we also thought he had dressed up his little effort to make it look better.

Sometimes, instead of making a good look better, the dress-up makes the bad look less bad.

I think of an AA business meeting where a long-time member verbally assaulted a one-year sober member of the Group who had put his hand up for a service position. The long-timer demanded to know if the young member had read the AA service manual and understood his responsibilities. He left the poor volunteer quivering and unlikely to volunteer for a service position again.

After the meeting, the long-timer said to anyone who would listen, "We senior members have to ensure that our trusted servants know the rules."

He had dressed up his bad behavior to look better.

In the Program, we undress our behaviors. Conducting a written inventory as outlined in Step Four, with the pen-to-paper discipline and, confessing to another human in Step Five, we reveal our behaviors for what they are. It strips our behaviors of the clothing we put on to make our good look better and our bad look less bad.

Undressed, our characters and behaviors stand naked; we see the good as merely good and the bad for what it is. Then we can get to work.

PART FOUR

Resentments

Webster's and Oxford Dictionaries agree on this definition of resentment: Resentments are feelings of bitter indignation arising from perceived harms or wrongs.

Here are some GEMS touching on this prickly subject.

Imagine, Imagination

At AA meetings, we hear some outstanding shares.

The other day a young lady topped them all. She introduced herself and opened with, "Imagine... a resentment."

She paused as we puzzled over this for a moment.

Then she explained, "Yesterday, I developed a huge resentment over something that happened a couple of days ago. It is still with me today, and it still irritates me."

She paused again, taking a sip of coffee, "But that's not the problem. The problem is, I am not sure it ever happened."

Everyone in the room laughed, and everyone who laughed understood that they were laughing at themselves. Each of us had created resentments in our minds. Each of us had experienced a resentment and wondered later if the offensive act had really occurred.

Often, when I do an inventory, I am surprised and say to myself, "Imagine... a resentment." Then later, I wonder, did I "Imagine... a resentment."

My memory is both short and creative.

Naughty or Nice?

It was December, near Christmas.

At our AA meeting, Step Eight was the topic. We were talking about making a list of people we had harmed, a list of amends to be made.

The first person to share was a lady who had attended our meeting for several years. She said, "I always think of Step Eight at this time of year. I think of Step Eight as the Christmas Step. I am making a list, and checking it twice, going to find out where I was naughty, not nice."

We laughed out loud.

It was a good and merry Christmas for us AAs.

Caragana Resentments

I was talking with a sponsee, talking about resentments. I wanted to make a point about resentments, how they were challenging to remove and blocked us from the world. How removing them required an outside power.

We were standing on the sidewalk next to a tall and dense caragana hedge. It was a perfect prop to make my point; I said:

> This is a caragana hedge. They grow quickly and have strong, deep roots.
>
> At our first house, we had a caragana hedge; it was a vegetative wall. I could not see the street from the house, and you could not see the house from the street. We were cut off from the neighborhood. I was isolated.
>
> One day, I decided enough was enough.

I pruned the hedge back so that I could see the street. The barrier was shorter, and trimmed to be neat. I was pleased. I could see the street and, sitting on my porch, I felt I was part of the community.

But caragana is resilient; it quickly grew back. Before I knew it, the house was cut off from the neighborhood and the resurgent hedge was shapeless and messy again.

After several cycles of trimming and growing back, I decided I did not want the hedge anymore. I cut it to the ground. But it grew back faster than ever. Finally, I called a contractor with a backhoe, and he dug the deep roots out. The hedge was finally gone.

My resentments were like a caragana hedge. They separated me from the world and the world from me. And my character defects were deeply rooted.

I tried to manage my resentments with inventories and amends, I trimmed them back, and I connected with the world, and the world could connect with me. But, like the hedge, they came back stronger than before. I cut them back hard, right to the ground, and still they came back.

I had to call in external help; I called on my Higher Power and His spiritual backhoe. I asked Him to dig them out, root and branch.

I had caragana resentments. I could make progress by cutting them back, but to get rid of them, I had to ask God to dig down with heavy equipment and get at the roots of character defects.

With the resentments gone, I can see people, and they can see me. I am part of the neighborhood."

I groaned out loud when my sponsee replied, "I guess you can hedge your bets, but not your metaphors."

Plowing Our Defects

I had a friend. He farmed grain on several square miles of land, cultivating it for decades.

He was a careful farmer. He knew the details of his landholdings, the wet and dry areas and the acidity levels of each of the thousands of acres he owned.

He had a fertilizing and seeding plan, applying different fertilizer levels and seeding densities depending on the soil conditions. He also had a plowing program designed around the topography of the land.

There was a hill in the center of the farm; it rose gently from the flats. He called it the big hill. The big hill governed his plowing pattern. The flat areas of the farm were plowed in straight lines, and he plowed the big hill in circles.

Straight lines up and down the hillside would have created channels down the slope; any rainfall would have run off the hill and eroded the soil. Plowing across the slope caused rainwater to gather in the furrows instead of flowing down the hill, preserving moisture and preventing erosion.

As I said, a careful farmer.

One day, I visited the farm. His field was freshly plowed. "I see you finished your plowing for the year."

He replied, "Yup, this is the last year I have to plow the big hill in circles. Next year, straight lines for the whole farm. I will save a lot of work and time.

I asked, "Why the change?"

I had a topographical survey done when I bought the field, and the big hill was 90 feet above the flats. I updated my topographical survey this year, and the big hill is only 30 feet above the flats. After working the land all this time, the big hill elevation is 60 feet lower than when I started. Now the slope of the hillside is low enough that I can plow straight lines without any drainage problems.

"My years of plowing around the hillside wore the hill down. Each circular sweep of the plow moved a bit of soil down the slope. I did not see the difference from one year to the next but, over the decades, 60 feet, amazing.

"So next year, straight lines should save me two days of plowing, even more for fertilizing, and another two days of harvesting. I will save time and be more efficient."

Later, as I drove home, I thought about my life. I thought, plowing a hillside was an excellent analogy for my defects. For years I plowed the hills of my defects up and down, and life's rainfall ran down the slopes, deepened the furrows, and the hill remained high.

Finally, I asked God for help. He developed an orthogonal plowing pattern across the slopes. Instead of plowing up and down, I plowed my defects round and round. I protected the soil, preserved moisture, and gradually lowered the height of the defect hill.

Following His plan, I did not see or feel the incremental changes from one year to the next—the changes were small as each pass of the Steps moved a bit of character soil—but the pattern was relentless.

Every application of the Steps was another circular pass of the plow across the slope, and a tiny bit of the defect wore down.

Under God's plan, the erosion stopped, and the hill wore down. The defects were lessened and finally removed. And when they were finally removed, I saved time and was more efficient.

My friend was a careful farmer, and my Higher Power is a careful God.

Cheesy, Hollow…
and It Works!

One morning, on my phone app, I selected a guided meditation on "difficult people."

An argument from the previous day was still on my mind. I thought, "A meditation on difficult people would be a good idea."

The guided meditation began. After introducing breathing and mindfulness exercises, the meditation narrator said, "Imagine someone you love, someone whose presence enriches you."

"Darn," I thought, "I have misread the title; it was supposed to be a meditation on difficult people."

A sneak peek at my phone confirmed the title of the guided meditation, "Meditating on Difficult People."

Returning my focus to the meditation, I obediently imagined someone who made me feel good.

The guide continued, "Imagine this person seated across from you. See them in your mind's eye. What do you feel?" After a pause, he continued, "Acknowledge the pleasure that he or she brings to your life." He paused again. "Now bless them."

"Now," he said, "imagine someone who is slightly bothersome. Imagine them seated across from you. See them in your mind's eye. What do you feel? Acknowledge the feeling of negativity that they bring to your life. Be honest; you don't like them." He paused, then said, "Now bless them."

I thought, "That was not so easy."

The app directed me to focus on my breathing. Then the narrator resumed, "Now, imagine someone who is difficult, someone who has made you angry and upset; imagine your enemy."

My conversation from the previous day came easily to mind. The narrator continued, "Imagine him or her seated across from you. See them in your mind's eye. Bring your feelings forward. Be honest in your views; acknowledge your judgment and opinion. Express your thoughts about them."

I could see where this was going.

The following words were, "Now release those feelings. As you have blessed the others, bless them. Ask for the same blessing on your enemy that you give to your friends and others."

The narrator paused; then, as if he heard my thoughts, said, "Don't think about it; just say the blessing."

I thought, *how cheesy and hollow is this? Who do they think they are fooling? Not me. I could see through this charade.*

But I followed the directions. Though I did not believe my own words, I said, "I ask for a blessing for the son-of-a-gun."

I'll be darned—it worked. I arose from that meditation feeling better about the obnoxious twit. The proof of the pudding was in the eating. I saw him later that day. Instead of bitter anger, I felt only mild irritation.

For the next three mornings, I did the same meditation. My attitude towards my antagonist continued to improve. I progressed from mild irritation to an impartial sense of goodwill. And I began to see that he was only a twit, not an obnoxious twit. Still later, I realized he was just difficult, not a twit.

It turns out that cheesy and hollow are pretty effective.

PART FIVE
Our Higher Power

A m I truly interested in my Higher Power? Sometimes yes, but sometimes, no.

How important is my focus on God? Sometimes very, but sometimes, not.

Interest and importance are two qualities of mind that help relate to God. These GEMS zero in on our attention and discipline in seeking and nurturing our interest in an important relationship with our Higher Power, as we understood Him.

Experiencing Our Higher Power

Quoting an outstanding share at the Akron Group, "You don't know God; you experience God."

What a profound insight. We cannot know God, but we can experience Him.

Thank goodness Bill did not say, "God, as we *know* Him." He said, "God, as we *understood* Him."

With the word *understood*, Bill points to our experience with God rather than our theories about God.

My connection with God is not intellectual, it is experiential; it is not theoretical, it is practical. If I remember this distinction, I avoid the volumes of debate between sects and religions. Instead of arguments about theories of God, which divide, in AA, we share our experiences of God, which unite.

As a fellowship, AA is remarkably united. We have not broken into sects, principally because we share our experience of a Higher Power in our lives, not our thoughts and theories.

Focusing on our experience of God rather than our thoughts and theories turns us to our stories of God. This is good because no one can argue with stories. All someone can say is, "That's not what happened." And the straightforward reply is, "Well, you were not there."

In the Fellowship, when we share our stories of how a Power greater than ourselves has worked in our lives, we are on the same page, even when it seems outlandish. For example, recently, an AA sister shared her story.

She said, "I asked God to find me a parking space."

Though I was puzzled by the idea of a Higher Power being involved in traffic management, I could identify with her connection with God, expressed in this anecdote. In the story, I could see a meaningful and tangible relationship. Someone who relies on a Higher Power to find a parking space has a connection with God which is alive and real. My stories don't involve parking spots, but they do show a connection with a Higher Power that is real and alive. Therefore our stories were, at some level, the same.

Another example comes to mind. I have discussed spiritual growth with an AA friend who is an avowed atheist. I shared my experience; working the Steps, my bearded man in the clouds idea of God had been replaced with an ineffable presence in my life.

He shared that by working the Steps, he was coming to feel a flow in the universe.

We disagreed on our theories of God, but we agreed on our stories of experiencing a spiritual flow. I can share my experience of the presence and flow of God and relate to an atheist who experiences a flow and power in the universe.

Experience and sharing our stories are the keys to this unity. With experience and stories, we are united; with theories, we are divided.

Program vs.
Sex, Reputation, and Wealth?

What would happen if I applied myself to spiritual development like I applied myself to sex, reputation, and wealth?

As a young man, I enthusiastically chased girls. If I fancied a young lady, I worked hard to catch her eye. Her interests became my interests. I would focus and concentrate on her with single-minded determination. (Fortunately, the fun was in the chase; I was not very successful.)

As a lawyer, I dedicated myself to enhancing my reputation. I worked twelve-hour work days. I would listen to clients with patience, endure lengthy meetings, and concentrate on drafting documents for hours. I was fully engaged in building a reputation.

As an investor, I focused on making money. I paid attention and focused my attention on our investments. I pored over reports and analyses and had long meetings with management. I was utterly absorbed in the pursuit of wealth.

I have pursued girls, reputation, and wealth with single-minded focus and passion, going to great lengths with discipline and energy. I pursued them assiduously because they were important to me.

You would think my spiritual life and my relationship with a Higher Power would be at least as important as girls, career, or money. But, all too easily, I put matters of the spirit in the back seat. I do not bring the discipline, focus, and drive to my spiritual life that I bring to other activities.

For example, it is easy to forget morning prayers and meditations. In contrast, I never lost track of a girl. During the day, I lapse in focus on my Higher Power, but I never lost focus on my legal practice. And spiritual values catch my attention for short moments, unlike the complete absorption I gave to making money.

I do not bring the discipline and focus to my spiritual life that I demonstrated in my quest for sex, reputation, and wealth. The facts indicate that spiritual matters are, for me, less important than girls, reputation, or wealth.

If I worked half as hard on spiritual matters as I did on either sex, reputation, or wealth, the Dalai Lama would be sharing a stage with me, and both Tony Robbins and Deepak Chopra would be seeking me out for advice.

Thankfully, with age and experience, spiritual growth is becoming more important to me; it is a growing higher priority.

Just Pray –
Talk on Your Knees

At a AA meeting, the topic was prayer.

A young man caught our interest when he said, "Because my sponsor is not here, I can share a story."

We wondered where this was going.

"I had a big problem and I was pissed. Madder than all get-out."

"After I described the problem and how it was affecting me, my sponsor thought for a moment, then said, 'Every morning, get on your knees and talk about the person and situation.'"

"I told him, 'You know I don't believe in God. Why would you tell me to pray? It would be dishonest. And besides being dishonest, it would be unhelpful; how does kneeling and talking to God resolve my problem? Is He going to fix it?'"

Our friend quoted his sponsor's reply, "I didn't say that you had to get on your knees and pray to a God. Neither did I say that you had to believe in God. I said you had to get on your knees and talk about the problem. It's not complicated. Two things: First, you get on your knees; second, talk about the problem. And I did not tell you to ask that the problem be fixed; I told you to talk about it, nothing more. That is my advice. You can take it or leave it."

Our friend continued his story:

    I need a new sponsor, was my first thought. But I had a second thought—I have never gone wrong following his directions before; maybe I should try this.

So, I followed the dishonest and silly instructions.

And, goodness gracious, the problem dissolved over the next ten days.

How did my sponsor know that kneeling and talking into the air about my problem would work?

Well, I have given the matter some thought, and I think I know how he knew it would work.

First, when I got on my knees, I was physically reminded that I was not the highest power in the universe.

I googled "positions of prayer," and found out psychologists have learned that kneeling triggers unconscious attitudes and filters that cause me to unconsciously admit that I am not the highest power in the universe. As a result, I adopt a mental state of teachability and humility.

Second, by talking out loud about the situation, I had to structure my thoughts and articulate the elements of the problem coherently. When thinking and brooding inside my head, my thoughts were crazy, random, and irrational. My crooked and twisted thinking becomes straight and orderly when channeled into words.

Third, maybe there is a God, and perhaps He fixed the problem."

Our AA brother concluded, "Bottom line—if you have a problem, get on your knees and talk about it; it works. It really does."

We laughed when he concluded, "Because my sponsor is not here, I can share that story. He does not need to hear he was right again; his ego would get out of hand."

Best Share Ever

AA in Gulf Shores, Alabama is impressive. The slow southern language and the welcoming hospitality make for brilliant meetings. And there is a cultural meme: You pass if you don't have anything to say about the Program and the solution and, perhaps because of the slow manner of speech, people seem to take time to think about what they are saying. As a result, shares tend to be concise and Program-based.

I have heard many outstanding Alabama shares, but one share at one meeting stands out. The subject of the meeting was meditation. The AAs at the meeting made several good comments which, following the Gulf Shores AA pattern, were short and Program-based. Some described various methods and styles of meditation. Others emphasized the importance of meditation.

Then came the turn of an older gentleman, well-dressed in a patterned shirt and beige slacks. He had a relaxed face, white hair, and weathered features, and he exuded a quiet calm that suggested years of serenity.

With a long southern drawl and a rumbling bass voice, he began, "Hi, y'all, my name is Marvin, and I am an alcoholic."

He paused. "Tonight we are talking about meditation. Well ... I have a little something to say on that subject."

After a long pause, he continued, "Meditation has nothing to do with technique and everything to do with discipline... Thank y'all, I'll pass."

What more could be said?

Don't Push, P.U.S.H.

Acronyms are fun, and good memory aids for sound principles of living. We can keep them handy, ready for immediate use.

At an AA meeting, someone reminded us of the acronym, P.U.S.H.: Pause Until Something Happens.

You can keep it handy in case of an emergency. Next time you are in trouble, don't push; instead, P.U.S.H.

As the mythical Saskatchewan farmer says, "If you are in a hole and want to get out, the thing first you do is stop digging." Often, in a crisis, we get busy doing the same thing with more enthusiasm and energy. Which is how we dug the hole in the first place. So we dig the hole deeper and faster.

Pushing against the problem, getting busy, and digging the hole deeper, makes things more difficult. The solution—don't push the problem, P.U.S.H. the problem; Pause Until Something Happens. When I P.U.S.H., I stop whatever I am doing and wait until something happens. At the very least, I'm not digging the hole deeper.

Could this acronym and strategy of Pause Until Something Happens get any better? Yes, it could. The acronym is improved with *Pray* Until Something Happens.

When I P.U.S.H.—Pray Until Something Happens—I am both paused and mindful of God. And there is nothing better than turning to God in a crisis. Things improve, guaranteed.

And thinking of the Saskatchewan farmer's advice on what to do if you are in a hole, if I pray, I am looking up, and, looking up, I see how to get out of the hole.

Prayer is an excellent addition to an already good acronym. So P.P.U.S.H.—Pray and Pause; do both. And to remind myself of the whole thought, I pronounce the acronym with a short stutter, *p-push*.

Curiosity is Great

I arrived at the coffee shop early for a sponsee meeting. Sitting near the front window, I saw him drive up and park across the street. He got out of his car, locked it, and turned to walk to the coffee shop.

Another driver, parked next to my sponsee's car, was standing on the sidewalk. I couldn't hear what was said; I could only see what transpired.

The other driver said something and pointed at my sponsee's car. Within seconds they were angrily yelling at each other. Finally, after much arm waving, they parted, and my sponsee stomped across the street to the coffee shop.

My AA brother walked into the shop, got his coffee, and sat down. I wanted to give him some time. So we discussed several items on our sponsorship list before turning to the sidewalk incident.

I asked, "What was that all about?"

Recalling the temper tantrum, he said, "He started yelling at me about how I had parked my car, and I started yelling back. I don't know what his problem was."

He paused, thought for a moment, then said, "Isn't that interesting? I did not know what his problem was. And thinking about it, it would have been better if I had been curious when he challenged me. It would have been better if I had stopped and asked myself, *why is he so upset?*"

What a powerful insight. We talked about this new idea and agreed, curiosity is an excellent attitude for any conversation. In a difficult conversation, asking ourselves a question is a great idea, and any question will work.

We can ask ourselves, "Why is this happening?", "What is he saying?" or "What will she say next?"

We agreed, if we are curious, we are mentally and spiritually open to possibilities rather than reacting to situations. With a questioning attitude, we adopt an attitude of humility and, with humility, we are halfway to acceptance. And with acceptance, there is no fight.

We carried the idea further. If we start with an attitude of curiosity, we are ready to listen. It triggers interest in what will be said. And that is always a good rule to follow; be interested, be mindful.

This trick will work anywhere and anytime and is particularly helpful in spousal communications.

Frequent Contact Is Better Contact

The women were in a marriage workshop.

The workshop leader asked, "How many of you love your husband?" All the women raised their hands.

Then she asked, "When was the last time you told your husband you loved him and needed him in your life?"

Some of the women answered "Yesterday," a few said "Last week," and some couldn't remember, but they were sure it was "recently."

Then the leader told the women to take out their cell phones and send the following text to their husbands, "I love you and need you in my life." Next, she instructed the women to exchange their phones and read aloud the replies.

Here are some of the replies from the puzzled husbands: "Who is this?", "Yeah, I love you too; what's wrong?", and my favorite, "I thought we agreed you wouldn't drink during the day."

This story is both funny and makes a point. It is a point about communication in a marriage, and there is a lesson about communication in the spiritual realm.

I can see myself in a seminar on spiritual development and the leader asking, "Do your love your Father in Heaven." I would, of course, raise my hand. Then the facilitator would ask, "When was the last time you told God you loved Him and needed Him in your life?" Of course, "recently" would be my reply.

But what would be the reply from heaven if I could text my Higher Power, saying, "God, I love you and need you in my life"?

If I rarely tell God I love Him and need Him, then the answer from heaven will be like answers from the husbands; "Who is this?", "What have you done now?", "How much do you need?", or "I thought we agreed you wouldn't drink during the day."

But if I express my love and need for Him frequently, He will not be surprised and puzzled, like the husbands in the story.

Sign Posts

Asking God for guidance is one thing. Seeing the answer is another. What does God want me to do? How can I know it? Does He send a memo? Do I get a text? Often there are many correct paths to follow. Which one should I take?

I was working with a newcomer years ago. He wondered he if should go to a treatment center. Back and forth, back and forth; go, not go, go, not go.

At first, he wanted me to make the decision. I declined, reminding him that he should pray and ask for knowledge of God's will in this matter. To this suggestion, he replied, "That hardly seems practical, how will I know the answer? Should I watch for a finger writing on the wall, or will I see a cloud and hear a booming voice?"

I said, "In my experience, God will give you signposts. Ask Him for knowledge of His will, then watch for the signposts as you move forward. God will set up way-finding signage to point you right."

He seemed doubtful. But agreed he would try.

That was Saturday. Wednesday, he called and reported, "I was looking at a treatment center's website, and they have a place open."

I thought, "This sounds like a signpost," but said nothing.

Thursday, he called, "You know my father and I don't get along."

"Yes," I replied.

"He just called out of the blue. I told him I was sober and going to AA meetings. He said he would pay for a treatment if I wanted to go."

"Well, that is interesting," I rejoined.

"Yes," he said, "It's amazing." We signed off without further comment.

Friday afternoon, he called and said, "Oh my God, my managing partner just left my office. He said he had heard I had a drinking problem and was getting some help. He wanted to tell me that the firm was 100% behind me if I needed any time to take counseling or treatment."

I agreed that it was remarkable.

Saturday, we met for our regular session. He started with the treatment question—go or no go. He said, "I am still waiting for directions from God."

I was silent, then replied, "Let's review the last week."

"Wednesday, you confirmed that there was an opening in a great treatment center. Thursday, your dad called and agreed to cover the costs. Yesterday, your managing partner told you he knew that you were dealing with an alcohol problem and that if you needed time off to get your act together, he would cover for you."

I paused and asked, "How many signposts do you need?"

After a pause, my young friend replied, "You have a sarcastic tone in your voice."

I apologized for sounding sarcastic.

He went to the treatment center. He's still sober today.

Over the years, time and again, I have learned to ask God for knowledge of His will for me, continue forward, and watch for the signposts. They will appear.

Churches May Be God's House

We love our holidays in the Deep South of the United States of America.

I recall one day in particular, in the South Carolina Lowcountry. It was a meandering drive on a two-lane blacktop road through farming country, cotton fields, and corn. Windows down, we could smell the soft, warm air.

My wife, driving the car, slowed as we entered a village. It was like a postcard from the TV village of Mayberry, a clean and orderly country scene, the main street with a character restaurant, drug store, and a few other shops. Each store was well-kept and tidy. I expected to see Deputy Barney Fife sitting outside the barbershop.

We pulled into the gas station to fill up.

I got out of the car, walked around to set up the pump, and commenced my fill. With the nozzle in the gas tank, I squeezed the handle to start the flow and locked it in place. The pump bell chimed as the tank filled.

With nothing on my mind, I looked over the car's roof. The service station was attractive, art-deco, out of the 50s. The exterior was white with bright green trim, two service bays and an office. The garage doors were open, and I could see into the service bays. A mechanic was working on a car.

The space was neat and tidy, all the tools laid out, ready for use, cans of fluids neatly stacked—even the oil stains on the floor looked clean. Everything about the space suggested purpose. This was a serious workshop, dedicated to automobile maintenance.

The gas pump clicked off. As I turned to put the gas nozzle back in its slot on the pump, I looked across the road, and the village church came into focus. It was a beautiful sight.

The green-grassed lot was well-groomed. The church building was perfectly situated on the landscape. The simple, white structure showed through the green leaves and gray Spanish moss. The architecture was balanced; the windows were proportioned to the building. The steeple, seen through the branches, was topped with a cross.

Everything about the building confirmed its purpose, which was boldly declared on the sign at the front, "This Is God's House." Then I noticed a small blue AA circle and triangle sign on the side entrance.

A share from an AA meeting came to mind: "Churches might be God's house, but his workshops are meetings of Alcoholics Anonymous." Two buildings, an attractive art-deco garage and a beautiful church, and both had serious maintenance workspaces.

I turned and looked back at the mechanic in the workshop, the service bay of the garage, and decided to call my sponsor.

Meet My Future Wife

I was meeting with four AA brothers for a morning coffee. We were reviewing our day ahead, sharing our plans for the day, and reminding ourselves to watch out for self-pity and dishonest or self-seeking motives.

One of our members, recently divorced, was feeling depressed and alone. He said, "I miss being married. Today, I am going to pray that I meet my future wife."

One AA brother cautioned, "Be careful what you pray for; you might get someone like your last wife, which did not end well. You better be specific; you should ask for a good wife."

Picking up the theme, a second AA brother chimed in, "Good point, but why stop there? If you are going to tell God what you want, you could ask for a wife who is good and rich."

I said, "While you are stipulating your specifications, she might as well be pretty."

Our fourth AA brother laughingly said, "One thing is becoming clear: Even the simplest prayer gets complicated if we start outlining the solution. Maybe you should leave it to God and ask for the wife that He would have you marry."

It was a humorous interlude, one of the advantages of a small gathering of old friends.

Later, my friend called and said, "The exchange this morning was great; it reminded me not to put boundaries on God's grace."

PART SIX

Change

C hange, changing and changes, all three verbs are challenging and necessary. Here are some GEMS on change.

How Were You Affected?

We could not desire to stop drinking until we knew we were drunks, and we could not desire to live a spiritual life until we knew we were unspiritual. Before choosing to get better, we had to know we were sick. To be restored to good, we had to know our bad.

And for us AAs, we come to know these things with a written moral inventory.

In the Big Book, we find the famous four-column inventory format. Following that process, first, we make our grudge list, writing names of people, institutions and principles that "made us angry" or "burned us up." Then we outline the facts which led to these names being on the grudge list. After getting the facts down, we turned to our reactions. We asked, "How did this affect me?" and "What was my part?"

For the answers to these questions, I let my mind flow freely. I don't pause to think; I let it flow. No reflective wordsmithing, just writing. I pick up my pen and start writing—a free-flowing brain dump, writing down thoughts and words that come to mind.

If your experience is like mine, as you let it flow and write down how things affected me and what was my part, certain specific words show up again and again.

These repeated words and phrases reveal patterns in my life and character. Patterns I would have denied before starting the inventory process.

I recall the surprise of my first inventory. Partway through my third column writing, a hateful phrase flowed onto the paper. I stopped. I realized this was not the first time I had written this phrase. I looked back over the preceding pages. I had written theses hateful words five times.

Two things came to mind: First, I said to myself, "That is not me; I don't think like that." Second, after a pause, again to myself, I said, "There it is in black and white." I had to face these attitudes and realize I had some nasty beliefs and attitudes buried deep inside.

And seeing these phrases I had written down, I knew what I was, and I was not too fond of it. But seeing these defects, I was prepared to change.

In all my inventories, I have been surprised at the patterns revealed; the free flow of thought, combined with pen-to-paper, seems to expose what is really going on in my heart. The words tumble out onto the paper, allowing my dark and brooding unconscious to emerge. Then, and only then, I can see what I am and what needs to change.

Defect Removal Worksheets

AAs have an appetite for change, good change. This is not just a theory; it is a fact.

We reviewed the4thdimension.ca website traffic statistics which show which pages were opened and which materials were downloaded by AAs looking at the site. We study these statistics to identify the parts of the website generating the most interest.

The most frequently opened and downloaded materials are the Defect Removal Essays and Worksheets. These are serious worksheets that involve change at the depth. It surprised us that these were the most frequent downloads; we did not expect the heavy-lifting materials to be the most popular. There appears to be an appetite and desire for change amongst AAs using the website.

We ought not to have been surprised. Starting with our drinking, we first learned that change is possible and positive.

With our Program life working the Twelve Steps, we followed a disciplined and constructive change management process. Our first change was the cessation of drinking as the result of our initial spiritual awakening. We liked the ending of drinking and our first spiritual awakening; therefore, we applied the Steps in all our affairs and experienced more positive changes and spiritual awakenings. Our fear of change grew to tolerance of change grew into a desire for change.

A close second to the Defect Removal Essays and Materials in downloading traffic are the Morning and Evening Checklists. The same rigor and discipline found in the Defect Removal materials are also found in the daily habit of using Morning and Evening Checklists. AAs have learned the value of a morning and evening review of the day, a disciplined process that informs and guides our thoughts, which lead to actions, which lead to habits, which build a character.

The popularity of the Defect Removal Essays and Worksheets, followed by the Daily Checklists, amongst the users of the site reflects their embrace of the discipline of our change processes.

Visit the website: the4thdimension.ca

Inches and Yards

The subject of the meeting was "removal of defects."

One AA brother shared, "I am happy God works with me in inches, not yards, because by the inch, it's a cinch, but by the yard, it's hard."

He continued:

> I had been reading the Big Book for years before I realized that the Seventh Step and the Seventh Step Prayer were not saying the same thing.
>
> One night, someone read the Seventh Step Prayer at an AA meeting. I heard him read, 'I pray that you now remove ... every *single* defect of character.' The word 'single' leapt out at me and seized my mind. I was sure he had misread the Prayer. He should have said, "remove *all* my defects of character." When I got home, I looked it up. He had not misread the Seventh Step Prayer. There is a shift between the Step and the Prayer; the Seventh Step refers

to *all* our defects; the Prayer refers to *single* defects.

For years, relying on my faulty memory, I recited the Seventh Step Prayer, saying, 'I pray that you now remove ... all my defects of character.'

I had a warehouse of faults, and I expected that God would deal with all of them with one swipe of His heavenly hand. But that is not what the Prayer says. And that is not how He worked in my life.

God dealt with my defects one defect at a time, not 'groups' and certainly not 'all.' Instead of a great leap, God took an incremental approach, an easier, softer way. I am thankful that He paid more attention to the words of the Seventh Step Prayer in the Big Book and ignored my misremembered prayer.

I am thankful because it's a cinch by the inch, and by the yard, it's darn hard."

Living and Thought -
Less to Full

It was a great meeting. Someone raised the slogan "Think, Think, Think" as a topic for discussion. Several AAs talked about thinking before drinking, others talked about thinking before speaking. Those were good shares. Then one fellow raised the bar.

He started by agreeing with everyone who had shared so far, then tacked to another direction:

> In my drinking life, I had slogans. The best was 'Don't Think, Don't Think, Don't Think.' That slogan applied to my drinking, which was a thoughtless habit. My first drinks were always thoughtless, without thought. In fact, it was important that there be no thought; if I thought about what I was about to start, I might remember what happened last time and stop. My drinking was thoughtless.

And thoughtlessness was not limited to drinking; I lived thoughtlessly. Utterly self-possessed, I would do things with no regard for anyone else. Mindless anger or rage were my "go-to" reactions to life. I would explode if I thought that I did not look good or the world was not behaving as I thought it should. I never thought; I reacted.

My drinking was an example of this. If I thought, if only for an instant, before taking that first drink, I would have remembered the last drinking episode and how it worked out and stopped before I started. This thoughtlessness was just an example of my whole approach to life.

Sobering up and coming to meetings, working on the Steps and helping newcomers, I have begun to think about life and what it all means.

This is affecting everything, my whole life. Expressions like 'To thine own self be true' and 'An unexamined life is not worth living' now mean something to me.

'Think, Think, Think' means that I have Thought, Thought, Thought about life and what it all means.'

His share caused me to reflect on my pre-Program life and the changes the Steps have brought. My AA brother was right; sober and working the Program, I live a thoughtful sober life, in contrast to my thoughtless drinking life.

Navigation Awards?

I grew up on Lake Superior, and sailing was a family activity during the summer. Dad bought his first keelboat when I was 11 years old, and overnight cruises and day sails were frequent.

At the end of the sailing season, the local yacht club held a banquet when the boats were put away for winter. At the annual banquet, awards were given.

One year my father received the "Navigator of the Year" award. The presenter described him as a great navigator with detailed knowledge of Lake Superior.

Dad accepted the award with his customary grace and humility. He referred to the praise the presenter lavished on his navigation skills and explained, "The praise for my navigation skills is not warranted; any knowledge of the Lake that I possess came hard and at great expense."

He paused, then elaborated, "What appears to be skilled navigation is merely knowing where the rocks, shoals, and reefs are located, and I know where they are because I have hit each of them... often more than once."

The crowd laughed.

Recently a sponsee I was working with said, "You have such knowledge of the Program... you seem to know how to navigate life."

I replied, "Your praise is not warranted." Channeling the memory of my father, I elaborated, "Praise for my navigation skills is not warranted; any knowledge of life that I possess came hard and at great expense. What appears to be skilled navigation is knowing where the rocks, shoals, and reefs are, and I know where they are because I have hit each of them... often more than once."

My sponsee laughed.

Do, did; Get, got

" If you always do,
What you always did,
You will always get,
What you always got."

This little ditty is part of our Program life. It could be a slogan poster at our meetings.

It is quoted to newcomers. But the poem's value applies to old-timers as well.

Storming around the house when I don't get my way, does not work any better after years of sobriety, than storming around the house while drinking. Gossiping about my co-workers over lunch will trigger hurt feelings and betrayal, even after years of not drinking. Justified self-righteous anger is as damaging to an old-timer as it is to a newcomer.

It was hard to learn that doing the same things gets the same things, even after I had stopped drinking.

When I celebrated my third year of sobriety, I was a young power-driven lawyer. I was not drinking, but many of my old living habits persisted. I was doing the same things and getting the same results. In my third year of sobriety, the results of demanding perfection from myself and everyone around me were no different from the results in my first year of sobriety. I was doing the same things and getting the same results. I was doing what I always did and getting what I always got—pain, misery, and angry reactions throughout the day.

It reached a crisis when the firm's office manager took me aside. She said, "There is no doubt that you are doing well, and secretaries like to work with winners, but your temper and tone are such that I cannot find anyone to work with you. The word is out. You might be a winner, but you are difficult to work with."

She paused to let that hard advice sink in; then, in a softer tone, said, "A new attitude is in order."

I was deeply grateful for her advice. She did not have the tools to show me how to change, but she could see the problem and had the wisdom to share her insights.

I had to turn to my AA sponsor and our Program's Steps for the solution. I had to inventory my behaviors, see the defects for what they were, then turn to my Higher Power to remove them.

The changes did not happen overnight; some were quick and some were slow, but eventually, I stopped doing what I always did. When I stopped doing what I had always done, I did not get what I always got.

Proof of the pudding is in the eating; my current assistant and I have been together for over 30 years.

It works; it really does.

Slow Learners and Fast Forgetters

We read "How It Works" at every AA meeting. Years ago, an AA history speaker told the story of how this started.

There was a woman in California whose husband was a terrible drunk. She knew of some other women who had alcoholic husbands. She heard about the Big Book and wrote New York for a copy. On receiving it, she read it and saw the light.

She organized a meeting of other wives who had besotted husbands, and they dragged their husbands along. The men met at their wives' command in a Los Angeles hotel meeting room.

The women gave their men their only copy of the Big Book and sent them into the room, saying, "This book is a solution. Read it; we'll be waiting outside."

The men gathered around a table. One of them took the book. Opening it for the first time, he turned to the Table of Contents. He said to the other men, "There is a chapter entitled 'How It Works.' It is the fifth chapter, not the first, but that sounds like a good place to start."

So the custom began. And now most groups read it at every meeting.

We in AA read "How It Works" over and over because we have learned the value of repetition. Alcoholics are slow learners and fast forgetters. We need this repeated touchstone. We need to be constantly reminded of the principles and processes of our Program.

Routine or Ritual?

Marketing experts charge hefty fees to find the best names for products. There is a good reason for this. The name of a product is important; the right one taps into the deep meaning of the product and will resonate with customers for decades. The best names carry all the promises and hopes of the product or activity. Think of "Juicy Fruit" chewing gum or "GoodLife Fitness" gyms. The best names are remembered with ease. And the best names frame the activities or products with positive memories and thoughts.

At our AA meeting last night, the topic was "daily meditations." An AA brother shared his experience with the importance of names:

> When I meditate in the morning, I am ready for the problems I can see; I am poised and balanced, which allows me to handle situations I do not see.

When I pray and meditate, life runs smoothly. It works so well, I begin to meditate daily. The habit persists, for a time, then one day, I think, 'I can forgo my meditation routine today.'

Who knows why I reached this conclusion? Maybe I am tired; perhaps I don't think I need it anymore. Whatever the reason, I skip it. After all, it's just a routine, a habit, nothing big.

Initially, nothing dramatic happens. So I skip another morning and then another, and soon I have lost the habit; the routine is abandoned. After about fourteen missed days, my life will be in the ditch. Remembering what it used to be like, I meditate again; I recover my daily habit and routine. About ten days later, I am out of the ditch and back on the highway of life, things are running smoothly again.

Over and over this happens; I lose the routine, reestablish it, lose it again, and so on.

One day, pondering this repeated pattern, I wondered: Maybe I was losing the routine because I was using the wrong name. Routine sounded like work; it reminded me of exercise and hard work. And it sounded mechanical. I decided to rename my morning quiet time. Instead of calling it a routine, I decided to call it a *ritual*. Ritual seemed more important and meaningful. It had a sense of sacredness. And a ritual seems more permanent than routine, and ritual resonates better than habit.

Like any good name, *ritual* tapped into the deepest meaning of the activity, it resonated in my heart and mind and brought forward the best memories of morning prayers and meditation.

Things seemed to work better when I call it a ritual. This may sound funny, but I have not missed a morning meditation since renaming it."

I tried it; I renamed my morning *routine* to a morning *ritual*. My AA friend was right; the name makes a difference. My morning "routine" is now my "ritual," and I have not omitted it once.

Ritual properly frames the activity; it is a good name.

Guides and Goads

Cattle are not ambitious animals. Left to themselves, unaware of farther and greener pastures, they will graze in the same place for a long time.

The cowboys looking after them know there is better feed in the next pasture, but they also know that you cannot motivate a herd of cows by standing in front of them, describing a vision of a better pasture. The cows only move when they are prodded from behind. Cowboys often use a sharp stick called a goad; they ride behind the herd, poking the cows with their goads.

And once the herd is moving, cows need guides. Fences, gates, and other barriers guide the cattle forward on the correct path.

Moving cattle to the next pasture requires both goads and guides.

Alcoholics are not ambitious animals. They will drink for a long time without moving. They have no awareness of further and greener pastures, like sobriety.

People around an alcoholic, the metaphorical cowboys, include judges, police, wives, and doctors. They learn that standing in front of the alcoholic, describing the benefits of sober life, will not get him moving to sobriety. Alcoholics need to be jabbed from behind with sharp sticks. The metaphorical goads include threats, interventions, and confrontations, all designed to motivate the alcoholic forward to sobriety.

And once moving, alcoholics need guides. Goaded towards sobriety and moving forward, alcoholics need guides to stay on the right course. Meetings, Steps, and sponsors are all guides to keep the alcoholic on track.

Guides and goads; cattle and alcoholics need both.

Welcoming Mistakes

A young lawyer and his mentor were having lunch. The senior partner enjoyed passing on his wisdom. And the young lawyer gained contacts, knowledge, and confidence.

It was a solid professional relationship. But this day, the young lawyer broached a personal subject.

He began cautiously, "We have always talked about professional and office matters; today I have a personal question. I hope you don't mind."

Curious, the older mentor said, "Sure."

Unconsciously demonstrating how serious the young protege felt about the question, he put down his cutlery. "You have had a great career in law, you are wealthy and happy, you have a good marriage and get along with everyone; it is obvious to anyone who knows you, you have succeeded in all areas of life."

After a pause, he continued, "Is there a secret you could share with me? Is there advice you can give?"

The mentor focused on cutting his meat while he pondered the question. He thought, "How can I answer this? I don't have a silver bullet. Each of us has to learn and find his own path."

Seeing an answer, he smiled and said, "That's a great question.

"The secret key to success is making right decisions, lots of right decisions."

The young man hesitated, then asked, "How do you know when you are making the right decisions?"

The mentor smiled as he replied, "You need experience, lots of experience."

The young man was puzzled. Every answer seemed to lead to another question. He pushed ahead, asking, "How do you get experience?"

With a twinkle in his eye, the elder said, "You make wrong decisions, lots of wrong decisions."

The mentor smiled at his own humor, saying, "Good decisions are built on bad decisions. I was not born with a knowledge of hot stoves; I had to experience a hot stove. I touched it, and it hurt. I was not born with the knowledge of parenting; I had to experience parenthood, which included many mistakes. But all that is obvious, not a secret.

"If there is a secret, it is this: All these lessons would have been lost if I had not been mindful and aware.

"Only if I am mindful and aware will wrong decisions lead to experience, which leads to learning, which leads to future right decisions. So the secret is to be mindful and aware."

The mentor was wise. We have to find our own path. We cannot be told how to succeed, we must learn, and learning takes experience; experience comes from mistakes and mistakes start with decisions, and this formula only works if we are mindful.

The Hula Hoop of Control

It was Tuesday night at our men's AA meeting.

The topic for discussion was acceptance.

There were several outstanding shares, but one member nailed it.

"When I was in treatment," he began, "we had group sessions every day. Our counselor used toys and props, emphasizing points with rubber ducks, play hammers, and hand puppets. He had used them all to good advantage—all except one, the hula hoop. We had been there several days, and he had still not used the hula hoop. We wondered when the hula hoop would be used and what point it would make.

"One day, a fellow inmate was complaining about the state of his life, his job, and the universe as he saw it. The counselor reached for the hula hoop, laid it on the floor in front of the fellow, and said, 'step into the hula hoop.' The complainer complied and stood inside the hula hoop.

"Standing back, the counselor said, 'Inside the hula hoop is all you can deal with; everything outside the hula hoop is out of your control. Accept it.'"

Everyone in the group thought it was funny and dramatically made the point. In the succeeding days, we would often say to each other, "That is outside my hula hoop."

Our AA brother continued his story, "That image stuck with me all this time. This afternoon I had a problem and imagined I was standing inside my hula hoop. Inside the hula hoop is mine; outside my hula hoop, it is out of my hands; accept it.

"So I asked God for some serenity and moved on."

We nodded in agreement; the hula hoop was a great visualization.

Gary, who shared his hula hoop story, brought one to the next meeting and donated it to the group.

Now a hula hoop is at the front of the room. If someone is complaining about this, that, or another thing, we hold up the hula hoop and remind him of the importance of acceptance.

From Fixing the Past
to Facing the Future

The company was in trouble; it needed a transfusion of cash immediately. But the negotiations for investing money in the company were stalled; the owners and investors both wanted control.

Running out of patience, the lenders called all the loans for the company. Bankruptcy loomed. The company had hit its bottom.

With everyone focused by the crisis, terms between the owners and investors were quickly settled. The former owners needed the crisis to ensure their cooperation. The investors advanced capital, took control, and began the turnaround.

But the bank calling the loan was only the first of many crises; every day consisted of one urgent problem after another. Suppliers, creditors, and customers were all upset, and each demanded attention. Employees panicked and needed to be reassured. There was no end of problems.

Weeks one and two were a whirlwind of 24-hour days, everyone putting out fires.

Weeks three and four were busy, but productive. No new fires exploded, and some old ones were cooling down. The team spent time assuring customers, bankers, and staff that the company would survive. The suppliers were given some money. The banks got comfortable with the new situation. Employees became confident they would keep their jobs.

The storm was passing. Management was able to focus more and more on the operations and customers.

By week five, a new normal was emerging; the Chief Financial Officer presented his first cash flow forecast, which showed how the company could move forward. The President laid out his plans for revised operations.

With each passing week, the yelling and shouting reduced, and the business felt more regular. The company was transitioning from fixing the past to focusing on the present.

At about week six, management presented a marketing strategy for a new product line. It was a good plan, and the investors could see advancing more capital into the company to make it work. The company was now facing the future.

This completed the cycle. The company had hit bottom and desperately fixed its past, then transitioned to focusing on the present, and now they were facing its future.

That is the nature of business turnarounds: Hit bottom, fix the past, focus on the present, and face the future.

It is also the nature of sobering up.

First, the alcoholic must hit bottom, which is necessary to ensure he gives the required cooperation. This is a time of crisis, a lot of yelling and shouting and general panic, and new fires are exploding all around.

But the alcoholic discovers AA, and the process of recovery starts.

First, there is a period of fixing the past and making amends.

Then we identify defects and begin their removal with our Higher Power. We are focused on the present.

One day, we realize that we can look to the future. We have come into alignment with our Higher

Power and desire to improve our characters and grow spiritually.

In sobering up, we hit bottom, move from fixing the past to focusing on the present, and then face the future.

Turning around a business is a lot like turning a drunk around.

PART SEVEN
Life - Experience

L ife is lived experience, and sober life is sober experience Experience is sometimes felt, sometimes inflicted, sometimes earned, sometimes given. Internal or external, experience teaches us if we are honest, open and willing. Experience, happy or sad, pleasurable or painful, can be lessons or losses. The choice is ours.

I hope you enjoy these meditations on life and experience.

Program Puzzle

My wife loves getting flowers; they are like a magician's wand. She could be in a blue funk on a winter's day, and a surprise bouquet of lilies will have her smiling from ear to ear.

This is puzzling for at least two reasons. First, the flowers seem to small compared to her attitude change, which is so great. Second, I can see no rational connection between her feeling better about life and receiving flowers but, based on my experience, the reaction is highly correlated and predictable.

Fortunately, I don't have to understand the connection between flowers and attitudes to get the benefits; I just have to do it.

My AA Program, like flowers for my wife, is puzzling. And as with the flowers puzzle, there are two reasons for the Program puzzle.

First, like flowers for my wife, there is no correlation between the magnitude of the effect to the magnitude of the apparent cause; doing the Steps seems tiny compared to the changes I experience, which are great. The relief I experience—relief from a seemingly hopeless condition of addiction and the relief I experience with increasing emotional sobriety—is enormous; all in return for a few simple Steps.

Second, again, like the flowers, I can see no rational connection between the Steps and long-term, contented sobriety. Taking time from my busy schedule to meditate should cause stress and anxiety but, when I meditate, I become peaceful. Dredging up my past should cause shame and guilt, and confronting people I had harmed should drive me to drink but, when I do these things, I am more serene

I don't understand the connection between the Twelve Steps and a better life but, like flowers and spousal attitudes, they are highly correlated and predictable. I don't have to understand why these things work, I just have to do them.

I buy flowers for my wife and reap the benefits; I do the Steps and reap the benefits.

Make the World Work for Me

For those of a certain age, memories of John F. Kennedy are strong; memories of a modern Camelot and the age of Aquarius.

I recall watching Kennedy's inaugural address on black and white TV. The day of the inauguration was overcast, and the wind was cold. Despite the weather, the crowd was eager and looking forward to a new generation of leadership, the youngest ever President, a President for the hip generation.

Everyone expected a great speech, and he did not disappoint; he was a skilled orator. In his inauguration speech, he called on all Americans to think and act differently when he said, "Ask not what your country can do for you, ask rather what you can do for your country."

This dramatic and powerful statement has been repeated again and again. It is compelling and memorable, a phrase that defined a presidency.

The president knew oratorical tricks. He understood the power of making a statement and turning it back on itself to highlight the lesson to be learned. That phrase reversal is a powerful rhetorical flourish and is part of the reason we remember it so well.

I heard a share at a recent AA meeting that used the same technique.

Quoting my AA brother, "I demanded that everything work out the way I wanted. I demanded happiness from the world. I pointed this out to God, and God replied, 'Ask Me not to make the world unfold for you; ask rather, what can you do to make My world unfold for Me.'"

God has some rhetorical flourishes of His own.

Level Up

My young sponsee was wrestling with a defect of character.

He said, "I am struggling to level up."

"What," I asked, "is leveling up?"

He thought for a moment, considering how to explain a videogaming term to a 70-year-old.

After gathering his thoughts, he said, "Leveling up is a term used by videogamers. Videogame designers build in ever-more-challenging levels of play and, at each level, he gives the gamer powers to deal with the problems found at that level. When a player defeats a dragon or completes a task at one level of play in the game, he is given new powers and is allowed to play at the next higher level. With the new powers earned at one level, he can match the more powerful dragons and more challenging tasks at the next level.

"When he completes a level and earns the new powers, he has *leveled up*."

I grasped the analog immediately. The young sponsee was striving to defeat the dragons and defects presented at this level of sobriety, he was striving to *level up*. Defeating the defects and dragons at this level of sobriety, he will have proven himself ready for the more demanding challenges and tests of the next level. And with defects removed and his spiritual condition enhanced, he will possess new powers from his Creator, powers necessary to meet these more difficult challenges.

The balance of the conversation focused on the demons and dragons he was facing, it was a great session and he was leveling up..

Later, reflecting on the conversation I thought, everyone living a Twelve Step life *levels up*. We start where we are, then, "as the result of these Steps," we have a spiritual awakening. We have a spiritual awakening and experience "victory over our difficulties," earning new spiritual powers. Then life moves to another level. At this new level, we can meet the increasingly complex challenges and tests presented with our new powers. Powers granted by "God, as we understood Him" in the levels passed so far.

Our Higher Power is the game designer who gives us what we need to meet all challenges at each level of life.

If we were to re-write the Big Book using younger language and jargon, Step 12 might read "Having leveled up as the result of these Steps...." The Step 3 prayer might read, "God, please help me level up by giving me victory over my difficulties." And Steps 6 and 7 might say, "We humbly asked for the weapons and powers to level up."

And while we are re-writing the Big Book, we can launch a new video game, Grand Life Sober.

My Ego is a Bad General

If I am not careful, my ego will take command of my life.

"Command" is a military term; when I think about command and commanders, I think about generals, and one of the experts on generals was Napoleon.

Napoleon was asked, "What makes a great general?"

He replied, "There are four kinds of general. The best are smart and energetic; they are smart enough to know how to properly handle any problem, and they are energetic enough to get the job done. The second-best are smart and lazy. They are smart enough to know the right thing to do, but they are too lazy to get it done. The third-best generals are stupid and lazy. Their decisions are stupid, but they are too lazy to get anything done, which is a blessing. The fourth and worst, the very bad generals, are stupid and energetic. They get a lot done, but what they do is usually wrong."

My ego loves to take command and dictate orders like a general. And it is stupid and energetic, a type four general, a very bad general, the worst sort of commander of my life.

Full of energy, my bad general ego, makes stupid decisions; it does not respond to situations; it reacts and reacts quickly. It triggers powerful retaliatory actions and words from everyone around me. And my bad general ego is energetic; it issues commands, and things happen; time is spent, resources mobilized, and forces marshaled, all in the wrong direction. And all the bad decisions are implemented forcefully.

In summary, when my bad ego general is in command, things go quickly, powerfully, and rarely well.

What is the solution? Military leaders have learned bad generals must be replaced. They must be relieved of command and a new general appointed. I have learned the same lesson. My ego general must be relieved of command and a new general installed.

And almost any new general is an improvement over my ego, the type four stupid and energetic general.

The new commander, might be the Fellowship, my group, my sponsor, or any power greater than myself. He might be smart and energetic, smart and lazy, or stupid and lazy. Regardless, the new general is a better bet than my ego. And that is what the Steps are all about, learning to relieve my ego of command and appoint a new general in its place.

And practicing all of our Principles in all my our affairs, many of us turned to God and appointed Him as our new commander. He is smart and energetic, the best kind of general.

Guaranteed.

Failure Can Be Gold

The young couple, only months into their marriage, had words.

The new husband, an AA brother, thinking, "My wife is unmanageable," called his sponsor, who had been happily married for many years. They met for coffee and, after a brief preamble, the young husband asked, "You and Marg seem to be very happy. If I am not prying, could you share any tips on managing my wife, pointers to success in a relationship?"

His sponsor laughed, "I might have some thoughts, but you should be asking George. He would have some great insights."

Surprised, the young man responded, "Why would you point me towards George? He has gone through four wives. I heard him joke that he was tired of the marriage divorce treadmill. He was not going to get married again; instead, he would find a woman who hated him every few years and buy her a house. He has a great sense of humor, but relation-ship advice, maybe not so much?"

With a twinkle in his eye, his mentor said, "Correct; he is a great example of what not to do. That is his value; we alcoholics seem to pay more attention to lessons of failure than lessons of success. It seems easier to learn what not to do. And the failure that gives the lesson does not have to be yours; it can be his. The lessons are still there.

"And by the way, that is one reason to go to meetings. When you go to meetings you hear from the guys who go out drinking and come back; listen and learn from them. In relationships and drinking, failures are good lessons, and they don't have to be your failures to be your lessons."

Others Pay the Price

The other day an old AA friend, cleverly reframed the well-worn AA saying, "We go to meetings to find out what happens to people who don't go to meetings."

We were chatting about the shares at a recent AA meeting we had attended. My friend focused on one share in particular; a fellow who was returning to AA. He told how he had been sober for a while, drifted away from the Program, and started drinking again. We both chuckled when we recalled his rationale for the slip, he had said, "I wanted to conduct another experiment to prove that I was an alcoholic."

It was the usual wreck of a slip story. He lost his job, license, and wife, and came back full of remorse, pain, and self-pity. He had found a new and deeper bottom.

My AA friend observed, "I hate to admit it, but I almost look forward to attending meetings and hearing from fellows coming back from a slip. I see the wreckage and pain and am reminded again of the horrific consequences of drinking. Listening to and talking with guys who have failed, I learn what not to do and the consequences of failure. Their bottoms keep me sober. I have heard a lot of slippers like the fellow last night; they pay the price, and I get the benefit, I stay sober."

Then he quipped, "You could say, a lot of guys have paid a terrible price for my sobriety."

As I said, the usual wisdom, cleverly reframed.

When Have I Completed Step Twelve?

The meeting topic was Step Twelve.

One fellow asked, "How do you know when you have completed Step Twelve?"

There were several insightful shares: "We never finish Step Twelve, we continue to carry the message to other alcoholics," "Step Twelve is a lifetime practice," and "Step Twelve is not a Step, it is a way of living."

The general theme: We never finish Step Twelve.

Then the last fellow pivoted the discussion to a more interior view; he said, "I don't know when I have completed Step Twelve, but I sure know when I am back at Step One."

That share "rang my bell."

I recalled working with my first sponsor. We worked through the Steps. As the result of taking these Steps, I had a spiritual awakening. It was not a full awakening, just enough for me to stop drinking and stay stopped. It was my *abstinence awakening.*

Life was good; I was thriving and prospering. Not drinking was working for me.

But, if you sober up a drunken horse thief, you still have a horse thief. In my case, if you sober up a drunken perfectionist, you still have a perfectionist.

After many personal inventories, which revealed my demand that everything around me be perfect, I had to admit I was powerless over this unreasonable demand of reality—my life was unmanageable for this defect. I was at Step One.

It seemed to make sense to apply the principles and Steps of our Program to this problem of perfectionism.

Looking back at my inventory, I said, "I admit I am powerless over my demand for perfection—my life is unmanageable."

Then I applied the rest of the Steps to this problem; I applied the principles of the Program. I came to believe that I could be restored to sane or clean thinking in this matter. I turned this specific problem over to God, *as I understood Him. And based on my experience with Him and the relief form my drinking obsession, I understood Him to be an effective agent of change.*

I did an inventory around this issue and asked God to remove the defect of perfectionism.

I made amends for the harms I had done in demanding perfection of the world and everyone around me. And this process of applying the Steps to this problem worked.

Since then, I have applied the Steps to other areas of my life, including sex, sports, and work; and to activities such as smoking, eating, and other escapes. I admitted Step One for each of these matters, then worked through the rest of the Steps with a focus on the problem. And repeated this process with defects of character my inventories revealed.

In this way, I learned to apply Step Twelve, to apply the principles of the Program to more and more of my affairs.

I agree my AA brother; I am never sure when I have completed Step Twelve, but I can tell you when I am back at Step One.

You've Gone Too Far

One day, driving in the country, I stopped in a small rural village, I was looking for a particular farm and stopped in the village to get directions. I walked over to the general store.

The store was old— a screen door, worn wooden floors, and period lighting. The merchandise was well-ordered, and well-tended. It felt like the best of country living, where life was relaxed and easy. I looked forward to talking with the storekeeper behind the counter.

"Hi! It sure is hot. Glad to offer you some cool air and shade from the sun?" was the greeting from the old fellow behind the counter.

Wanting to honor the situation by purchasing something, I agreed with his observation about the heat and asked for a cold soda. As he made my change, I asked, "Do you know where the... farm is?"

"Well, yes, and I suppose you want to know how to get there," was the laconic reply.

"Yes, if you could."

"Well, it's easy; you continue down the road in the same direction you arrived. You'll go down a while. It's on your right, about ten minutes if you follow the speed limit, less if you don't. It's not well-marked. So, watch for it with great care.

"And if you come to the corner where the old oak tree used to be, you have gone too far."

Later, as I drove down the road, I reflected on the instructions. In particular, I recalled the storekeeper's warning, "If you come to the corner where the old oak tree used to be, you have gone too far." I laughed out loud. How would I recognize a corner where a tree "used to be?"

Then I thought, I used to give myself the same instructions when I drank.

As I had my first drink, I would think, "I will drink till I feel good. Then I will stop. I will watch for the good feeling with great care because it's not well marked. And I will know that I have missed the stopping point and have gone too far if I come to the corner where the old oak tree used to be."

Whenever I drank, I never recognized that damn "corner where the old oak tree used to be." I always went too far.

What Happened Before What Happened Happened

An AA brother shared, "When I was drinking, I would often wake up hungover and wonder *what the hell happened*?

"When I came to AA and began working with my sponsor, I realized the important question was not what happened. That was easy. Getting drunk was what happened. The important question was, what had happened before I got drunk. The important question was, what happened before what happened, happened?"

He paused and took a sip of coffee.

> Feeling restless, irritable, or discontented, I would take a drink. The drink solved the problem of these feelings. But I had an allergic reaction to alcohol; I got very, very drunk.

Looking at my history, I saw, taking a drink and getting drunk was the same as sniffing pepper and sneezing. Both were bodily reactions that I could not control. I could not solve the bodily reaction. I cannot inhale pepper and not sneeze; I cannot take a drink and not get drunk. I had to focus on the problem that preceded the bodily reaction, the sneeze or the drunk. I had to avoid inhaling pepper to not sneeze, and avoid the first drink to not get drunk.

My solution to the feelings of restlessness, irritability and discontent was a drink, and that first drink caused the drunk that happened. That is what happened before what happened, happened.

Seeing what happened before what happened, happened, I saw that I needed a different solution, something other than a drink. And the AA Program gave me a different solution. Applying the tools of the Program, I could ease my restless, irritated, and discontented feelings. I did not have to take the first drink to solve those problems, I could stop what happened before what happened, happened."

His share resonated with all of us. We had all discovered a new Twelve Step solution to being restless, irritated or discontented.

But it did not stop there. This Twelve Step solution worked on other feelings and emotions. It handled the big three of restlessness, irritation, and discontentedness; it also dissolved feelings like shame and remorse and dispelled emotions like guilt and anger.

And this process of discovery progressed. With good inventories and identification of the exact nature of what was happening, I could see and stop more things that happened before what happened, happened. I began to see the underlying causes of many of my mysterious damaging feelings and emotions. I began to see what happened before what happened, happened in all areas of my life.

These damaging feelings and emotions just seemed to happen. But if these happened, I could work on what happened before that happened.

Working the Program, I saw things that used to baffle me. Applying the Principles of the Program in all my affairs, I understood what happened before what happened, happened. And with this understanding, I could avoid the first drink, harsh word, emotional reaction, or bad behaviour. And without the first, what happened before what happened, happened never happened.

Spiritual Parapraxis

Confusing one word for another is not a modern spell-check problem; it has been a problem for a long time.

Parapraxis, or a *Freudian slip*, is a mistake in the words we use. Some believe that these slips of the tongue reveal unconscious thoughts. A slip of the tongue reflects a mental image that the speaker is trying to hide. Because the slip may have a deeper psychological significance, we refer to them as Freudian slips.

For example, a newsman reporting on a story about Prince Harry and his wife in California described him as the "douche of Windsor." When a Prime Minister of Britain, David Cameron, was asked about recent tax cuts for the wealthy, he replied, "We are raising money for the rich." Tiger Woods, the famous golfer, suffered a back injury; he had a bulging disc. A sports broadcaster reporting the story said, "Tiger Woods has a bulging dick."

Parapraxis, a slip of the tongue, can lead us to wonder what is going on in the speaker's mind.

AAs suffer from Parapraxis.

Recently an AA brother, reading How It Works, said, "I was powerless over alcohol, and my *wife* was unmanageable." Of course, the correct reading is, "...my life was unmanageable." He may have completed Step One, but he might see issues on the home front when he gets to his inventory.

Another brother, reading the Ninth Step Promises at the end of the meeting, said, "We will *instinctively* know how to handle situations." The correct word is intuitively. Instinct is a thoughtless reaction, while intuition is a mindful reaction.

Every once in a while, you will hear at the end of the Serenity Prayer, "My will, not thine, be done." The reversal of God's role and mine is apparent.

The most common slip might be in the reading of Step Twelve. It is a small slip, hardly noticeable. The reader will often say, "Having had a spiritual awakening as _a_ result of these steps." The correct reading is "Having had a spiritual awakening as _the_ result of these steps." If we do the Steps, a spiritual awakening is a certainty; it is _the_ result of the Steps.

It is not a probability or one possible outcome of many. The Steps are aimed at *the* result, which is a spiritual awakening.

We don't sober up because we have an unmanageable wife; our life is unmanageable. Before we are halfway through, we will not instinctively react; we will intuitively know. And it works better if Thy will is done rather than mine.

Lastly, if we do these steps, we will awaken spiritually, no ifs, ands, or buts.

"In My Way" Was in My Way

The meeting topic was Step Three, "turning our will and our lives over to the care of God."

An AA sister opened with a puzzle, "'In my way' was in my way."

She elaborated, "We in AA talk a lot about doing the next right thing. But we sometimes overlook who decides what the next right thing should be.

"When I think about Step Three and turning things over to God, it seems clear that God should decide the next right thing. But for years, I felt He had better things to worry about than what I was doing. To save Him the effort, I would determine the next right thing; I would do it my way.

"I thought this was the way to run my Program. I was focusing on doing the right thing. I had heard so many AAs in the Rooms describe their success in living by choosing the next right thing; I was convinced that holding that thought was all I had to do. I was aiming for the next right thing, not the next wrong thing; what could go wrong? And, of course, my intentions were pure.

"All these thoughts hid the problem; I was choosing the next right thing; I was still in charge, not God. I would carefully consider all relevant factors and balance all competing interests. But it was still my choice. I was choosing the next right thing *my* way.

"So, 'in my way' was in my way to finding God's way.

"Alcohol is cunning, baffling and powerful, and so is my egoistic thinking.

"But, thankfully, God is more powerful and patiently persistent. When I finally admitted that 'my way' was in my way of finding God's way, all I had to do was abandon my thinking and allow God to step in."

We all nodded in agreement. We had all been there again and again.

Smacked Upside the Head

Gulf Shores, Alabama, also known as Redneck Riviera, is our favorite holiday spot.

This story is another outstanding share from a Gulf Shores AA meeting.

The meeting was organized around a circle of tables. Well-established with a long history, the meeting included many old-timers. The meeting opened in the usual fashion. The Secretary asked if there were any newcomers. A young man raised his hand and admitted that he was coming back from a slip.

As usual, everyone perked up, and the meeting pivoted to meet the slippery returnee's needs. The shares focused on early recovery, working the Steps, and the need for a good sponsor.

We were halfway through the meeting. A middle-aged AA brother with an Alabama drawl introduced himself as an alcoholic. He said, "I had some slips before I finally got a sponsor and began to take this program seriously."

Then after a pause, which in the south is not a gap between words, but a paragraph between thoughts, he continued,

> I have been a carpenter for a long time. Years ago, I was apprenticed to a 'good old boy,' and he was tough. Whenever I made a mistake, he would smack me upside the head.
>
> "I had been on the job for a week, and I had been smacked upside the head several times. I asked him, why do you do that? Why do you hit me like that?
>
> "Well, this is what my boss told me; he said, 'I could put my hand on your shoulder and look you in the eye and say, don't do that again, that is naughty. But you wouldn't remember because you are a thick-headed, slightly dense redneck. For you, I do something memorable.'"
>
> Our AA friend wrapped up, "When I came to AA, I did not take it seriously enough. I went out drinking again.

"God could have told me that I was naughty, and I ought not to do that again, but I would not have remembered because I was a thick-headed, slightly dense redneck. So, God arranged for some serious negative consequences. He smacked me upside the head.

"It sure hurt. But after enough slaps, I finally got the message, and I have been sober ever since. Thanks."

As he sipped his coffee, we laughed, remembering our experiences of God giving us a loving "smack upside the head."

I Don't Know

In their famous AA talks, Joe and Charlie highlight the importance of saying, "I don't know" when working in the Program. But saying "I don't know" is good practice anywhere and anytime.

I was a young lawyer in a specialist firm. We had been called in to advise the trustee in a massive bankruptcy. My boss, the senior partner on the file, asked me to join the first meeting of the major creditors.

There must have been 40 people in the board room: bankers, creditors and all of their lawyers. There was a gabble of tense conversation in the room. Everyone was on edge. The amounts at stake were massive, and competing interests were emerging. Several of the bankers were claiming the same property.

The bankruptcy trustee called the meeting to order.

The first argument erupted almost immediately. Two creditors were at odds, and one of them was angry. Pointing at my boss, he demanded an answer to his aggressive question.

My boss had an unsurpassed reputation as a bankruptcy lawyer. In meetings like this, he was usually treated with respect and deference. But this creditor was angry; he cared nothing for my boss's reputation.

The room was quiet; the first of many shots of the battle had been fired. My boss was silent for a long moment; then, looking across the boardroom table to the angry creditor, he said, "That is a great question, and this is a difficult problem, I don't know the answer. We will get back to you with an answer and copy everyone."

He turned to me and said, "Make a note of that question; it is a great question."

The angry questioner calmed and visibly preened; he had stumped the great bankruptcy expert. And the meeting continued in an orderly manner.

After the meeting, we reviewed the tasks we had to complete. I reminded him of the creditor's challenge and the promise to give him an answer.

He said, "Thanks for reminding me; we should follow up with him. Please give me a memo on the point, and we can discuss it before sending it out.

"But, while we are talking about that, there is an important lesson I would like you to take to heart: Never be afraid to say, 'I don't know.'

"When you say, 'I don't know,' you gain the respect of every blowhard in the room for having the courage to say what they know they should say more frequently. And when you admit you don't know one thing, people unconsciously conclude you know everything else. They can't help it. Without doing anything, you gain influence and respect in the room.

"And, as you noticed this morning, you disarm an angry questioner. Suggesting he posed an important and difficult question will make him feel better and cost you nothing."

He concluded, "Be sure to write up a memo answering the question, copy everyone, and remind them of what a great question it was."

The lesson was a good life lesson: Never be afraid of saying, "I don't know."

Fearlessly saying, "I don't know" can be a powerful tool in your arsenal.

PART EIGHT

Automotive Program Thoughts

D riving and automobiles are a rich source of metaphors for life and sobriety.

Skid Marks

This GEM is a story, in a story, in a story.

I called my sponsor about an argument I had with my wife. We met for coffee.

He said, "Describe the conversation."

"Well," I said, "I politely offered some constructive comments. My tone was gentle and kind. I was only partway through making my points, when, without warning, she became angry. Then I became upset. We started shouting at each other. Then I left."

Then he told me a story. I was accustomed to this; he often answered problems and questions with stories.

The story he told was a courtroom story, about a trial following a car accident. He began, "The lawyer in this story asked the driver to describe what happened."

" The driver said, "I was driving at the speed limit and saw the other car move into the intersection, in my path. I immediately slammed on the brakes. But I could not stop despite standing on the brake pedal."

The next witness the lawyer called was an engineer who specialized in accident reconstruction.

The engineer took the stand and the lawyer asked what he had done to study the accident The expert explained he had examined the accident site and the damage suffered by each car from the collision, and calculated the speeds of each car at the point of impact.

The lawyer referred to the evidence of the driver and said, "The driver said he was driving at the speed limit, saw the other car and slammed on his brakes." The lawyer then asked, "What does the evidence you studied tell you about this recollection; does his recollection square with the facts?"

"Well," said the engineer, "there were no skid marks from braking, which you would have expected with a sudden stop, and, analyzing the crumple damage to the other car, I concluded his car was moving at least 80 kilometers per hour at the point of impact, much more than the speed limit of 50.

'Based on the evidence, it is clear that he was driving well above the speed limit and ran into the other car without touching his brakes. His recollection of what happened would seem to be mistaken.'"

My sponsor told me this story, then said to me,

Let's look at your recollection of the conversation with your wife—your spousal accident scene— and compare that recollection with the facts.

"You think you offered helpful comments in a loving tone, and, for no reason, your wife became upset. And you immediately began shouting.

"The conversational skid marks, her response to your comments, and your immediate anger suggest to me that your helpful comments were not welcomed and your tone was not loving and kind.

"Looking at the evidence, a reconstruction engineer might conclude your recollections about the conversation seem to be mistaken."

Damn sponsors, damn reconstruction engineers.

Nipigon Road Trip

We were teenagers, and four of us decided we needed a road trip. We decided on lunch at a diner in Nipigon, about 40 miles away.

One of the guys had a car. Laughing and joking, we piled in and took off.

The car was an old beater. It once had been a good car, but it had been driven hard; the years and miles had left their mark. The noise level was impressive and did not inspire confidence.

The fellow sitting in the passenger seat, in a loud voice to be heard over the noise, yelled, "The engine and transmission are making a lot of noise."

I added my two cents from the back seat: "It's not just the transmission; I think the muffler and exhaust are falling apart."

Our buddy, driving the car, grew tired of the criticism and said, "Don't worry, I can fix that."

He reached over and turned up the volume on the radio, way up. Shouting over the loud percussive rock music, he said, "There, problem solved."

We all laughed as we rattled and rolled down the highway.

But this is not merely a party story; it is a life story.

Drinking was like turning up the radio to drown out the noise of life.

When my friend's car was new, it ran fine, but he did not maintain it, and things wore out with age and miles. By the time of our road trip, it was a noisy beater. To hide the problems, he turned up the volume of the music.

My life was like my friend's car. When I was young, I was on a good life path. But I refused to mature and maintain my character. As I failed to grow up, to keep my spiritual condition, parts of my character began wearing out. And my life began shaking, rattling, and banging around. I was making a lot of noise as I rolled down the highway of life. To drown out the noise, I would drink. Drinking would drown out the problems and the bigger the problems the more I drank.

I came to AA and stopped drinking. I lost my alcohol radio; I had nothing to drown out the noise. The rattling and banging of my character defects were still present and active and, without the alcohol to drown them out, they could be seen and heard loud and clear. I could not hide them and could not hide from them.

With my defects revealed, I had to deal with them. With God's help, I began to work on a spiritual maintenance program and grow up.

I had to. And I thank God for all of that!

A New Car, a Spiritual Story

I purchased my first ever "nice" car. It was a brand-new Buick. I marveled at the sophisticated electronics. The sound system was a treat. It even parked itself.

I have never thought cars were important, I never give them a second thought. But suddenly there were many Buicks in the world. At stoplights and while driving I saw Buicks. In parking garages and parking lots, I noticed Buicks. Buicks were everywhere. They seemed to be attracted to me.

I don't think there was a sudden surge in Buick sales; I don't think there were more Buicks on the road than before. Neither did I believe there was some mysterious attraction force drawing Buicks to me. There was another explanation: This new car was important to me, and its importance in my life affected my perceptions of the world. When my Buick became important, it caused me to notice other Buicks and Buicks seemed attracted to me.

The world seemed different because my car was now important to me and my life.

This idea that we notice more and attract more of what we think is important is not limited to automobiles.

When I am anxious, I notice anxious people and they seem to be attracted to me. When I am angry I notice angry people and everyone I deal with seems angry.

When serenity is important, I see serene people and I am surrounded by serenity. When God is important, I will see reflections of His presence everywhere.

I have learned to watch what I am noticing; it is a reality check on what I think is important. What I am noticing and attracting is the real test of what I think is important, and it is not always what I think.

A new car and spiritual life have more in common than you might think.

When Drinking Had One Speed

An AA brother shared this automotive analogy.

He began, "Life is a journey in my spiritual automobile, and I am driving down the highway of life.

Before I arrived at AA, the journey was crazy. In my spiritual car, I was screaming down the highway, the gas pedal jammed at full throttle. The tachometer was red-lined. RPMs were off the chart. The sound was unbelievable. I was hanging on for dear life.

I only had one speed, fast. And fast had become scary. And my transmission would only do forward and reverse. Forward was anger. Reverse was fear.

The combination of the jammed throttle and the broken transmission was terrible. I was either screaming forward with anger or careening wildly backwards in fear.

If that were not enough, I had destroyed the clutch. Without a clutch, I had to force the gears from forward anger to backward fear. Shifting from forward to reverse meant slamming the shifter as hard as possible and grinding the gears through the change.

The lurching from anger to fear, at full speed, was violent. Everyone in the car—my family, friends, and co-workers—was thrown around.

That was my state when I came in. Full-speed anger or full-speed fear.

I needed a maintenance program for my life. And I had no mechanical skills or tools. But with help from my (Higher Power) mechanic and (Program) tools, I rebuilt my spiritual car. I started with the gas pedal.

With the gas pedal fixed and working, I had control of my emotional velocity. My emotional flow could be increased or decreased. I can still have excitement, but it is mindful excitement, not panicked excitement. And I can have fears, but they are not the full-on fears of my drinking days.

Next, I got a new transmission. The new transmission has three forward gears: *acceptance*, *tolerance*, and *love*.

And the clutch is now working; it is called *pause-pray-listen*. I can change gears and even back up without the grinding.

This newly repaired power train is better. Now my spiritual car can be navigated at slow speeds in tight parking situations and high speeds on the freeways of my life.

My spiritual maintenance Program and (Program) tools with my (Higher Power) mechanic have made life better.

But I must remember cars, and spiritual lives, wear out; my spiritual condition needs ongoing attention."

It was an apt share and a great analogy.

Cruise Control

I was at my regular AA meeting; relapse was the topic

An AA friend's share began at a curious spot.

He said, "Reading the news, you would think autonomous driving is something new, but I can assure you, self-driving vehicles made the news decades ago."

Taking a sip of coffee, our AA brother continued:

66 I remember this story like it was yesterday. It was the summer of 1971. There was a story in the newspaper about autonomous driving. A tourist from Europe had booked a recreational vehicle for a holiday. After receiving brief instructions, he took possession of the motor home and departed.

The tourist was impressed by the North American technology on his vehicle. It had a full kitchen, sleeping area, and reading chairs.

All the comforts of home. And a new amazing feature: He found a switch labeled "Automatic Cruise Control."

Taking the words on the label literally, he decided to see just how clever the vehicle was. He flipped the switch and removed his hands from the steering wheel and his foot from the gas pedal. It seemed to work; the car continued, maintaining its speed on the long straight stretch of prairie highway.

He let the vehicle drive itself for a few miles; the Automatic Cruise Control technology seemed to work. After seeing no problems in this small trial of the technology, he probably thought, "This is great; I can leave my seat and get a drink."

But he was not reckless. Taking one step at a time, I can see him standing beside the driver's seat, watching as the vehicle rolled down the straight and true highway, ready to jump back behind the steering wheel at the first sign of trouble.

So far, no problems.

Gaining confidence, he left the driver's controls and made his way to the RV's kitchen area, where the rescue team eventually found him. Because the inevitable happened—the prairie highway curved, and the RV went smoothly over the shoulder into the broad ditch, hit some soft soil, slowed dramatically, then gently rolled over, trapping our hero inside.

Fortunately, he had been able to brace himself. With the smooth off-road exit and slow rollover, he was stuck, but unharmed.

I do the same thing with my sobriety. I think that I have Automatic Spiritual Cruise Control.

Instead of paying attention, I let my sobriety look after itself. Thinking my program habits are no longer needed, I take my hands off the wheel and test the automatic spiritual controls. But I am not reckless. Prudently I stand up and watch, and nothing happens. Eventually, I walk away from the Steps and Principles of the Program.

Then life takes a curve. I traverse the shoulder, and, before I know it, I am in the ditch, where my sponsor usually finds me, far away from my spiritual tools.

Autonomous driving is not yet here, neither is autonomous sobriety."

PART NINE

Words & Principles

All we have is words; words are our tools for God's work. Everything we do is in words.

We tell stories, share experiences, and talk about hope and strength. We write inventories with words and discuss our defects with words. And we use words to speak with God.

With words, we can articulate principles— Program principles, life principles and living principles.

Principles and words are the tools we have. Here are some thoughts on words and principles.

Symmetrical Sobriety

Alcoholics of our type understand how much work and discipline is required to drink at an Olympian level; we were never thoughtless or casual about our drinking.

For us, drinking was a serious business involving thought and planning. Thought, to create drinking opportunities; planning, to ensure we did not run out once we had started.

I had a coffee with a newcomer. He had been in the Program for a few days. We talked about how much thought and planning we put into our drinking. We laughed as he described how he kept a special water bottle filled with Vodka in his golf bag. He did not like Vodka, but it was his drink of choice when he wanted to hide his drinking.

It was a good story; it suggested that he was "one of us." Anyone who put that much thought and planning into drinking while playing golf drank at an Olympian level.

He committed to working the Program.

Near the end of the conversation, he asked, "How many meetings should I attend?"

I answered,

> My sponsor taught me to go to as many meetings as days I drank. I drank three or four days a week; three or four meetings a week worked pretty well.

"But that was only the first part of his answer. He added an important point in that conversation, which I will share with you because it sure worked for me."

I continued, "He taught me a rule of Symmetrical Sobriety. The first application of that rule is that the number of meetings in a week should equal the number of days I drank. The second application of the principle of Symmetrical Sobriety was to take sobriety as seriously as I took drinking. He told me there was a symmetry between meetings and drinking days, and there was a more general symmetry between sobriety and drinking."

The newcomer was puzzled, "What do you mean? Besides the number of weekly meetings, how do you take the program as seriously as drinking?"

Reaching for an immediate example, I said, "Well, let's look at your drinking habits. You kept a hidden stash of booze in your golf bag; maybe you should buy a soft-covered Big Book and hide it in your golf bag? You could hide it like you hid your booze, and it would remind you to take your sobriety as seriously as your drinking.

"And it might be good to have a Big Book handy as you approach the 19th hole."

We Cannot and Can... Not Drink

A newcomer was attending his first AA meeting. Everyone who shared welcomed him and recalled their own first meetings.

One share stood out and concluded with something that caught my ear, something that the newcomer could remember, something we could all remember.

Our AA brother started, "Welcome to the newcomer."

He paused, then continued:

> I don't remember much about my first meeting, but I do remember everyone was friendly, and that was important because I did not have many friends then.
>
> I faced the mounting evidence of my drinking problem in the days and weeks leading up to my

first meeting. I had a lot of evidence to prove that I cannot drink: impaired driving offenses, divorce, and lost jobs. When I think back, I am amazed at how much evidence I needed to accept the obvious truth; I cannot drink. Maybe you can relate to that feeling—mountains of evidence that drinking is a problem. Trust me; we have all been there.

But admitting I cannot drink was terrifying. I could not imagine life without drinking. Was it going to be dull and joyless? What about business lunches, parties, and what if I got married? I would have to drink if I got married.

But I hung on to that one thing; I cannot drink. I remember thinking, well, I don't have to make a lifetime promise; let's try it for a while and see what happens.

Well, what happened was amazing. I came to meetings, got a sponsor, and started working on the Steps. And I learned that I can... not drink. I realized I could live without booze.

I will end with this; we learn we cannot drink, then we learn we can... not drink."

It was an outstanding share for a newcomer and everyone else. Simple and memorable. We cannot drink, and, to our great surprise, we discover, we can... not drink.

A Revealing and Unscripted Blurt

I was in Alabama at my Wednesday AA meeting. A speaker meeting.

The speaker told the story of a newcomer he met years earlier. The fellow was holidaying in Gulf Shores and had called AA for help. The central office in Gulf Shores passed him on to our speaker for a Twelve Step call. They met for coffee.

> He was a nice guy. And he was still shaky from the night before. Over coffee, his story came out.
>
> His wife had been complaining about his drinking for some time. She refused to go on this holiday unless he promised to behave. So he had promised he would behave, but forgot to tell her he might behave badly.

After a couple of days, he decided he could have an afternoon poolside drink. One drink led to many. The next morning she found him passed out on the deck. With no sympathy for his hang-over, she said, "Get help or get out."

He called AA, and the phone service passed him to me.

Coincidentally, my regular AA meeting of my Home Group was that night. My new pigeon agreed to come with me to the meeting. We chatted for a while longer, then went our separate ways. Later I picked him up, and we went to the meeting.

My Home Group meeting is small, and we have a good meeting before the meeting. There was joking and casual banter. We ensured our new friend had a Big Book and felt at home. The meeting began, and we all sat down at the table.

The chairman of the meeting suggested my new pigeon read How It Works. Everyone agreed it would be an excellent idea for him to do this, and he agreed. I opened his new Big Book to page 59 and pointed out what he should read.

He warned us that he had never read it before and apologized for any mistakes he might make, then commenced his reading.

It was a good reading. He finished the introductory paragraphs and began to read the Steps. He got to the Seventh Step.

He must have been reading ahead because he read the Seventh Step, hesitated, and exclaimed, "Jesus Christ!"

Catching himself, he apologized, then read the Eighth Step, where we promised to make amends to everyone we have harmed.

With this exclamation, our newcomer made a good point. Step Eight is a serious Step. We hear it read so often we take it for granted, but for him, it was the first time, and he understood the implications and work that would be required.

We sometimes gloss over the challenge of the Steps; they are serious and require effort, and sometimes it takes a fresh read to remember what is involved in our Program."

It was a great story, a dramatic reminder of how we forget how serious our Steps are. After many readings, we forget that we used to balk at them. We take them for granted and the seeds of complacency are sown

Seven Dwarfs

I can never remember the names of all seven dwarfs. I usually get five, struggle with the sixth, and hardly ever get the seventh.

Forgetting the names of the Seven Dwarfs does not have serious consequences. But forgetting parts of a list or series of actions can cause serious consequences.

Doctors have forgotten to get all the tools and sponges out before sewing up the surgery patient. Pilots have forgotten to lower the wheels before they land. Lawyers have forgotten vital steps, and their clients purchased property encumbered with inappropriate mortgages. These professions use checklists to remind themselves of the basic steps required.

Doctors review a checklist before the patient is closed up, counting the number of sponges and instruments that should be removed. Pilots have checklists to remember to lower the landing gear. Lawyers use checklists to remember to check the title on closing and ensure that the property you are buying has no inappropriate encumbrances.

For routine operations, which they have done thousands of times, professionals use checklists because they have learned, they forget.

Every morning I read spiritual material, meditate, pray, and review the day ahead. I do this every day. It is a simple list of things to do; how could I forget?

But I often realize partway through the morning that I forgot my prayer, meditation, or review of my day. This is my daily routine, which I have done thousands of times, and I have forgotten part of it.

Pilots, doctors, and lawyers resisted checklists for decades, claiming that checklists were for amateurs and they would never forget anything in routines that are so familiar. I fought morning checklists with the same thinking. How could I forget a simple series of actions? But I did forget and with distressing frequency.

Finally, I admitted that a morning and evening checklist would be a good idea, and went to the Big Book and looked at the questions on pages 86 and 87. There are two great checklists on those pages, one on awakening and one on retiring. I took those questions, developed a morning and retiring checklist, and printed them on a bookmark. (You can print my checklists from Daily Checklists at the4thdimension.ca/category/worksheets or order plastic-covered checklist bookmarks at the4thdimensionca.square.site.)

Now I don't have to rely on my failure-prone memory.

And if I needed proof of the failure-proneness of my memory, I could try to name all seven dwarfs.

(Grumpy, Dopey, Doc, Happy, Bashful, Sneezy, and Sleepy. I looked it up.)

Shame Is Not Humility

Step Seven and Humility were the topics of the meeting.

"Words are important," our AA sister began, "In the Program, I have to be careful to ensure that I understand the words I am using. Often my understanding of a word is too narrow."

She continued:

> Working the Program has expanded the meaning of many words.
>
> At my first meeting, my sponsor walked over and told me she was my temporary sponsor. That was fifteen years ago. I did not clarify what she meant by temporary. But I never imagined we would be together for fifteen years. I now know that temporary can mean up to fifteen years and counting.
>
> She told me I had to be always honest with myself.

One day I was upset with my husband. When she told me to forgive him, I replied, "No way. What he did was unforgivable."

She instructed me to fake it till I make it, to imagine that I had forgiven him until I actually forgave him. When I pointed out the obvious flaw, that I would not be honest with myself, she told me my understanding of honesty was too narrow.

I tried it, and it worked; now I know that being honest with myself includes dishonestly faking something till it becomes real.

Over the years, my sponsor has expanded the meaning of the words like temporary and honesty. The sponsorship is still good after fifteen years, and the dishonesty of faking forgiveness worked with my husband.

And another word she expanded was *humility*; she enlarged my understanding of the meaning of humility.

We were sitting in her living room with our Big Books and Twelve and Twelves. She read from her Twelve and Twelve, "Most of us have only a nodding acquaintance with humility."

"Well," I said, "I have lots of humility. I have been humiliated all my life."

She said, "That is not the humility we are interested in. You think humility means shame. That is one meaning of humility, but, in my experience, that sense of humility is selfish. We mean something different: we mean unselfish and other-centered humility."

She picked up her Big Book, and opened it and read an underlined sentence, "You get just a little sobriety, and you get just a little humility... not the humility of sackcloth and ashes, but the humility of a man who's glad he's alive and can serve."

That clicked. Shame, lack of self-esteem, and deep humiliation were the sackcloth and ashes that made me feel comfortable. Like a pig in her sty, I was wallowing in shame, remorse, and humiliation. I thought that was the only possible meaning of humility. My sponsor and the Big Book expanded the meaning of the word, the word *humility* includes a sense of self that makes me glad that I am alive and can serve others.

I said, 'Thanks, another expanded meaning.'"

Informal Check on Hearing

I talked with my sponsor and raised what I thought was a serious problem.

After I posed the problem, he said, "Let me tell you a story." He does that a lot. He began:

> A husband was golfing with his doctor. Walking down the fairway to the fourth hole, he turned to his doctor and said, 'I think my wife has a hearing problem. Can you recommend a good hearing clinic?'
>
> The doctor thought for a moment and said, 'Suggesting that your wife go to a hearing clinic is a bad idea. Let's try an informal hearing test. If the informal test shows a serious problem, call me. Then I can take it up with her on her next appointment. That way, you are not in the line of fire.'
>
> How would I do an informal hearing test?

'When she is in the kitchen, stand at the front door and ask a question. If she doesn't answer, move to the living room and try again. If there is still no answer, repeat the question in the dining room. If she has not replied, stand in the doorway to the kitchen and repeat the question.

'Where you are standing when she answers the question will tell us how bad her hearing is.'

The husband agreed; it was a good plan.

He went home. His wife was in the kitchen.

From the front door, he called out, 'What's for supper?'

Hearing nothing, he stepped into the living room and said again, 'What's for supper?'

Still nothing. Silence.

He moved to the dining room, 'What's for supper?'

Silence, still.

Now, worried, he stepped into the kitchen entrance and repeated the question, 'What's for supper?'

His wife turned and testily replied, 'For the fourth time... lasagna!'

I laughed at my sponsor's joke. It was a good one, and very appropriate to the problem I had raised.

Oh... what was the problem I had posed?

I had whined about unanswered prayers. I said, 'I am not getting answers to my prayers; I don't think God is hearing me.'

We all laughed, and each of us understood that God was standing in the kitchen and heard us from the front hall. His hearing is not the problem, it is ours.

Waves Are Emotions

My AA friend and I were sitting on a park bench, enjoying the ocean view, each with our own thoughts.

My friend cleared his throat and announced, "Waves are emotions, and tides are attitudes and perceptions."

Puzzled, I asked, "Where did that come from?"

Looking out over the harbour, he said:

> The winds of life create waves. You can see them. They start small, and, if the wind continues, the ripples will build up and become higher and higher. Waves are the water responding to the wind. But they are temporary. When the wind stops, the waves stop. The wind will blow and make waves; things will happen, and I will react emotionally. I can't do anything about that. But I know the feelings will pass. Like waves they will die down.

The winds of life can disturb my surface and make emotional ripples and waves. I can feel them, and my emotions change when the winds of life change. And when the winds of life stop, my emotions stop. They are impermanent.

Tides are another matter. Compared to waves, they are powerful. You can see waves, but you cannot see a tide. You only notice the beach grows as the tide retreats and shrinks as it comes in. And waves are temporary, with the wind. Tides are perpetual and regular.

Tides are my attitudes and perceptions. I don't feel them or see them. But when I start thinking the world is out to get me, the tide is out. Then later, I accept the world as it is, and I have some peace in my life. The tide has come back in.

The moon's gravitational force governs tides; my attitudes and perceptions are governed by my conscious awareness of my Higher Power. When the moon is close to the earth, the tides are large, and, when it is far away, the tides are weaker. My attitudes and perceptions change with my Higher Power proximity and awareness.

Tides will come in and out. If a tide is in, I know it will go out when the position of the moon changes. Sometimes the world seems like it is out to get me, and I need new attitudes and perceptions and, in those moments, I have to remember to change the position of my Higher Power in my life.

The psychic change Carl Jung described was like moving the moon's orbit circling the earth to change the tides. I needed a psychic change; I needed to change the orbit of God in my spiritual life. I needed to move my spiritual moon to have a stronger divine gravitational pull, a deeper awareness of my Higher Power."

We were silent again.

I sighed and thought to myself, "I am going to find someone less complicated to sit with."

Program Texting

It was a men's meeting.

The subject of the meeting was "How It Works."

The shares were outstanding. Men talked about how their lives had been changed by practicing the Program's principles.

But one share stood out from the others.

The AA brother took a sip of tea and introduced himself in the usual fashion. Then he held up his iPhone and said:

> I remember the first text message I ever sent. After I sent it, I called the guy to ensure he got the message. My wife thought that was funny.
>
> Nobody taught me how to text; I learned by watching others. I watched my grandchildren doing it, and it worked for them. I watched my coffee buddies doing it, and it worked for them. And I tried it myself, and it worked for me.

Now I text from my phone all the time. The phone takes my message as I tap on that tiny keyboard; it sends a radio signal and finds the right phone to receive the message. I do not understand how it works, and I don't need to understand how it works.

I watched others, saw them succeed, and imitated them. And now, texting is a vital part of my life; I can't remember how I lived without it.

When I came to AA, I was obsessed with "How It Works." I had to figure out how it worked. I questioned and argued with sponsors. What connection could there be between a physical allergy and a religious experience? I pointed out that there was no rational connection between a moral inventory and stopping drinking. I argued that harms done in the past were in the past and should stay in the past.

At meetings, I rolled my eyes at trivial and repetitive shares; I sneered at the slogans and sayings.

Life would have been a lot easier if I had followed the same path with the Program that I had followed with texting. All I had to do was watch what other AAs did and imitate them.

I do not need to know how texting works, and I do not need to know how the Program works. I have to follow the living examples I see in the Rooms of AA."

We all laughed. Each of us had had the same experience. We did not have to understand; we just had to do.

Visit Andy C. at
the4thdimension.ca

For more books, blog posts, podcasts,
printable worksheets,
and to subscribe to his weekly newsletter.

Crisis – Alcoholics Anonymous (AA)

The Starfish and the Spider is a management book that, surprisingly, includes an important discussion of AA and its future.

The author of this book analogizes organizations to spiders and starfish, suggesting that organizations exhibit, to varying degrees, the virtues and flaws of one or the other. In the analogy, the author focuses on the degree and nature of central control. Both spiders and starfish have central cores and outer limbs, but that is where the similarity ends and the author's point begins.

The author points out that starfish have a central body and arms radiating out. The central core controls the arms. But, he observes, if you cut the arm off a starfish, the starfish will survive and grow a new arm, and the severed arm will grow another starfish. Cut an arm off one, and you have two, each with the genetics of the original. Each arm has the multiplying capacity for independent life.

Spiders have a central body with legs radiating out. The central body controls the legs, but, unlike the starfish's arms, spider legs don't have independent generating capacity. If you remove a leg from the spider's central core, the leg dies. And breaking a leg off a spider can impair its functionality; remove a leg, and the spider will likely die.

Remove an appendage from a starfish, and you have two starfish. Remove a leg from a spider, and you will have none.

Most organizations have a central core with arms or legs, which are sometimes referred to as branches, cells, or groups.

Starfish organizations have central bodies and connected branches, cells, or groups. And as with a starfish, if you break off a branch, cell, or group, the original will survive and grow, and the broken away branch, cell, or group will not die; it will grow. As with a starfish, when you cut an arm off one, you will have two; in these organizations, sever a branch, cell, or group, and you will have two. And each new arm, cell, or group has the DNA of the original, and the newly grown branch, cell, or group can and will spawn yet another new branch, cell, or group. Because of this, starfish organizations grow quickly. It is impossible to kill a starfish organization by killing its branches, cells, or groups. It is, in modern management jargon, *anti-fragile*. It thrives in adversity and stress. Suppress the branches, cells, or groups, and they multiply.

Spider organizations, like starfish organizations, have central arms, which are also described as branches, cells, or groups. But unlike in the starfish organizations, the separate branches, cells, or groups radiating from the core must be connected to the center core to survive. Separated from the core, they are dead. And as with a spider, in such an organization, if you remove a branch, cell, or group, you can cripple or kill it. The hobbled organization limps along and then dies. And broken-away branches, cells, or groups cannot replicate the original. They are the opposite of the starfish anti-fragile; they are fragile.

The book describes two quintessential starfish organizations, Al-Qaeda and early AA. Organizations with opposite values. AA is love and Al-Queda is hate, but they have similar organizational characteristics. Both organizations are made up of independent branches, cells, or groups. In AA, we have groups and meetings; in Al-Qaeda, cells. In both AA and Al-Qaeda, cells or groups grow and subdivide. They spawn other cells and groups. If one is separated from the central core, the central core will continue to grow and thrive and the new breakaway will also increase, thrive, and replicate.

Any cell of both Al-Queda and AA was self-contained and self-administering. Shared values, embedded in their DNA, govern them. And the members see a purpose larger than themselves, for which they are prepared to sacrifice. These values and reward incentives align the members. No central coordination is needed.

The growth can be meteoric and, for both organizations, it was. And both AA and Al Queda are anti-fragile; they thrive in adversity.

Early AA was a starfish organization. Cut off a few members from a group; the original group would survive and another group would grow. Exponential growth was the result. With a shared DNA and only a loose organization, all members and groups were aligned with shared values and purpose, helping other alcoholics. The author points out that it was an excellent example of a starfish organization.

Spider organizations have different strengths.

Starfish organizations have positive attributes, resilience and growth. Directed from the center, there is great efficiency and profit. But they are fragile and lack the decentralized, democratic, and exponential growth that the anti-fragile starfish organizations possess. Spider organizations can move quickly and build complex engineered webs and structures. On the other hand, starfish organizations tend to be inelegant, clumsy, rough, and ugly. Their slow movement on the rocks and beach doesn't seem very productive.

The comparisons of the organization typologies correspond precisely.

The author highlights another aspect of the distinction between starfish and spider organizations: Some organizations which start as starfish change to spiders. Starfish organizations are sometimes cursed (or blessed) with property holdings and cash flow which will support a central controlling core. And the central controlling core can make persuasive arguments to enhance the move towards spiderhood. These arguments include efficiencies, standardization, and protection of core values. All these are true, and are self-serving to the central core.

The authors suggest that AA is morphing into a spider. Control from the center is growing—the New York office, with a multimillion-dollar budget, has evolved to become a controlling center for AA. The NY central office has asserted control in a slow evolutionary creep, with efficiency and maintenance of program standards as the justifications. The central authority is not yet a complete spider, but the shift to central command and control is present and growing.

I agree with the author's view. AA is becoming spiderish. The large central budget might support AA's spiderization, but the idea of central approval of the intellectual property of AA may have been the seed for this change. Conference-Approved literature may have been the beginning of the transition from starfish to spider. The idea that something could be and should be "Conference-Approved" was a crucial and initial part of the transition of AA from starfish to spider.

In the 1960s, the seed of central spider control was planted when our General Service body adopted the idea of Conference-Approved Literature. With this adoption, AA created the mechanism for a central authority to bless and sanction readings and literature. The justification for this decision was a classic spider argument: Standards had to be enforced to ensure that all AA groups were correctly developed. To protect the Program, no apostasy could be allowed. Central approval of the intellectual property would protect AA.

Accepting those arguments, AA began to lose its starfish capacities. And today, for AA's intellectual properties and organic capabilities, we have a central spider presence instead of starfish capacities, a central authority which approves literature.

Why is this important?

First, unlike starfish organizations, spider organizations lack exponential growth capacity. And AA growth has stalled. At least in North America, we don't see the remarkable growth from the 1930s through 1950s.

And AA thought on recovery is becoming fossilized. With central control of literature required, there are no new books, and simple pamphlets can take years to develop. Once at the forefront of addiction and recovery thinking, today AA lags.

We have lost the AA Founders' sense of adventure. Reading the history of AA, one can sense the willingness to experiment and try anything to see if it worked. Anything from tomato juice to psychedelics was fair game if it improved the chances of recovery.

We may be witnessing a decline in AA. Newcomers are not staying. Old-timers are bored. Central offices are closing with financial problems. AA runs deficits. Our precious AA is in crisis.

One decision made decades ago may have started the problem. The decision to have "Conference Approved" literature may have been the first step down the slippery slope to spiderhood.

Over the decades, "Conference-Approved" has become an AA mantra. In meetings and Central Offices across North America, if it is not Conference-Approved, it does not fly.

New ideas and approaches die in Inter-Group meetings, condemned by the phrase *it is not Conference Approved*. The bleeding deacons that Bill Wilson warned us of have new and powerful tools:

It is not Conference Approved.
"It is not in the Policy Manual."
"We looked at that, and New York has said no."

Service positions are only of interest to those steeped in "New York and Conference-Approved" language and ideas.

It need not have been so. If, in the 1960s, we had described the literature as *Conference-Supplied*, we would have affirmed Conference leadership and rejected Conference governorship.

But we did not. As a result, we are petrifying. Our literature and our habits are frozen in time. Our Founders' sense of experimentation and innovation has vanished.

We need to take AA back from the governors. Recently, I attended a meeting in a small village in Scotland. Remote from the Conference-Approved center of AA, the literature table included *Sermon on the Mount* by Emmet Fox and *Varieties of Religious Experience* by William James. They were displayed beside the Big Book, and *AA Comes of Age*. I thought, "What a refreshing literature table; various ideas and thoughts presented and allowed."

We need more literature tables and Central Office bookstores like Scotland's. We could start with examples of our Founders' canon, like the books mentioned above written by Fox and James. And we can begin by describing our literature as *Conference-Supplied* rather than *Conference-Approved*. It is a start. Let us have Conference-Supplied literature, no longer Conference-Approved literature.

Let us arrest the slide to spiderhood and recover our starfish nature. Let us start with an honest inventory of our mistakes, change our course, and recover our starfishiness.

From Frank Amos and His Report to John Rockefeller...

For some in AA, meditation and prayer are more important than meetings. But for most North American AAs, this prioritization of prayer and meditation has been lost in the contemporary AA culture of "90 meetings in 90 days" and "Meeting makers make it."

This is a short note on the importance of prayer and meditation in the founding days of AA. It is a story about Dr. Bob.

Dr. Bob worked with thousands of drunks in Akron. He was a prodigious Twelve Stepper. But, in the early days, he wasted a lot of time. He would spend as much as four or six hours with a potential alcoholic. But many, after hearing the message in these long conversations, declined to "follow our path." As Dr. Bob would say, "They were not ready to go to any length to get what we have."

Dr. Bob realized that the time he spent with these fellows could have been invested in working with someone who wanted what he had to offer. He determined to become more efficient in the use of his time. With this in mind, he developed a checklist, a protocol of commitments, to determine if a new pigeon was ready to hear his message. This checklist is found in the AA archives in a memo from a non-alcoholic.

As many AAs know, in the very earliest AA days, Rockefeller and his advisors were introduced to Bill W. and heard the story of this new recovery process and movement. They were impressed enough to send one of the senior advisors, Frank Amos, to check it out. Mr. Amos first met with the small group of New York AAs and then went to Akron to confirm the reality of this new sobriety society. He reported back with two memos to Rockefeller. In one of them, he discussed how Dr. Bob, the most successful twelve-stepper at that time, triaged the newcomers he worked with. He summarized the checklist that Dr. Bob and others in Akron used to qualify a new pigeon: a series of commitments were demanded of the newcomer before time, money, and effort were spent to bring him into the nascent fellowship. If the commitments were not agreed, the twelve-stepper would move on.

Paraphrasing the report, Dr. Bob's checklist consisted of seven commitments; five were described as essential, and two were optional. If the pigeon did not commit and agree to all five essential commitments, Dr. Bob would politely decline to spend more time with the fellow. He would wish the prospect well and move on. The optional commitments were, well, optional.

The five essentials were: (1) a complete admission that he was an alcoholic and could not drink again, (2) an obvious and heartfelt surrender to God, (3) a promise that he would work with others, carrying the message of sobriety and hope, (4) a promise of abandonment and cessation of all sinful activities, and (5) *a commitment to daily meditation, a daily morning devotion, and quiet time* (my emphasis).

The two optionals: It would be nice if he attended the AA meetings, and it would be nice if he went to church.

This explains why daily meditation is high-lighted as more important than going to meetings in both *Pass It On* and *Dr. Bob and the Good Oldtimers*. A commitment to daily meditation was one of the essentials required to qualify; meetings were optional.

Wow.

In the old days, they challenged newcomers to spend quiet time each day. And if the newcomer did not agree to a daily meditation practice, they moved on politely but firmly, explaining that daily medita-tion was required. They probably said, "If you want what we have, and are willing to go to any length to get it, then you are ready. But you are not, so keep drinking; you will become ready in due course."

In those days, AAs would have been puzzled if you said, "90 in 90" (90 meetings in 90 days), "Meeting makers make it," or "Keep coming back." Meetings were optional.

Daily meditation was required, meetings were optional. Maybe, instead of our modern admonish-ments to newcomers, we could be saying, "90 medi-tations in 90 days," or "Meditators make it," or "Quiet timers quit."

Maybe we need a "Back to the Future" moment.